Fine Motor Fun

Hundreds of Developmentally Age-Appropriate Activities Designed to Improve Fine Motor Skills

by
Sherrill B. Flora

illustrated by
Vanessa Countryman

Publisher
Key Education Publishing Company, LLC
Minneapolis, Minnesota

CONGRATULATIONS ON YOUR PURCHASE OF A KEY EDUCATION PRODUCT!

The editors at Key Education are former teachers who bring experience, enthusiasm, and quality to each and every product. Thousands of teachers have looked to the staff at Key Education for new and innovative resources to make their work more enjoyable and rewarding. Key Education is committed to developing and publishing educational materials that will assist teachers in building a strong and developmentally appropriate curriculum for young children.

PLAN FOR GREAT TEACHING EXPERIENCES WHEN YOU USE EDUCATIONAL MATERIALS FROM KEY EDUCATION PUBLISHING COMPANY, LLC

Credits
Author: Sherrill B. Flora
Creative Director: Annette Hollister-Papp
Illustrations: Vanessa Countryman
Cover Design: Annette Hollister-Papp
Editor: George C. Flora
Production: Key Education Production Staff

Key Education welcomes manuscripts and product ideas from teachers.
For a copy of our submission guidelines, please send a self-addressed, stamped envelope to:

Key Education Publishing Company, LLC
Acquisitions Department
9601 Newton Avenue South
Minneapolis, Minnesota 55431

Standard Book Number: 1-933052-78-3
Fine Motor Fun
Copyright © 2006 by Key Education Publishing Company, LLC
Minneapolis, Minnesota 55431

Contents

Contents

Introduction to Fine Motor Skills

Fine Motor Fun is a large educational resource written especially for early childhood professionals, kindergarten, first grade, and special education teachers, as well as occupational therapists. Teachers will be delighted with the wealth of instructional suggestions, ideas, and reproducible activities designed to help develop and improve fine motor and visual-perception skills of young children.

For some children fine motor skills are easily learned. Art projects and paper and pencil assignments are viewed as fun and rewarding. However, for many other children, learning how to color, hold a pencil, cut with a pair of scissors, complete a maze, or putting together a puzzle can become an overwhelming task.

The development of fine motor skills is necessary for learning how to read and to write. Children who have poor handwriting, find copying from the board difficult, struggle with low visual-perceptual skills, and have trouble identifying letters and numerals will benefit from daily fine motor instruction. Fine motor difficulties could actually be eliminated before they have even been identified, and children with identified fine motor difficulties may experience successful remediation.

All young children will experience greater success in school when they are provided with educationally sound activities that promote the development of fine motor skills. *Fine Motor Fun* can help all of the children in your class develop these important skills.

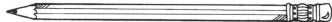

Definitions and Activity Ideas

Fine Motor Skills – This term refers to the ability to use the small or fine muscles that control the movements of fingers, hands, and wrists. Acquiring fine motor skills is necessary for learning how to properly use writing tools, scissors, and for the ability to throw and catch objects. Fine motor skills are developed as the neurological system matures and through time and practice.

Eye-Hand Coordination – In order for a child to develop effective fine motor skills, the child must also acquire the ability to integrate and coordinate visual information. Eye-hand coordination is a common term that refers to the child's ability to coordinate the information that is seen with what the child tells his hands to do. Eye-hand coordination is obviously needed for throwing and catching a ball. As the ball is thrown, the child must make visual judgements about how fast and how high the ball has been thrown, and then make an appropriate and accurate motor response.

The following are some fun ideas to help increase eye-hand coordination:
- Bat balloons to music.
- Use a toy bowling game and practice rolling the ball to knock down the pins.
- Play catch with a soft "Nerf®" ball.
- Play bean bag games and toss to a specified target.
- Blowing and then trying to catch or pop bubbles.

Visual-Motor Integration – In early childhood, young children use visual-motor skills to put together puzzles, stack blocks, and play with balls. Children are learning how to accurately reproduce shapes. They are learning to link what they see with what their hands are producing. Without the development of visual-motor integration, a child will find it difficult to learn how to reproduce proper letter formation. Be sure to provide many experiences where children have the opportunity to build with blocks, complete puzzles, or recreate patterns using pattern blocks or pictures.

Graphio-Motor Skills – This refers to any skill that involves using a writing tool. This includes coloring, drawing, and anything that requires crayons, pencils, chalk, or any other tool used to draw or write. Graphio-motor skills are also visual-motor skills.

Motor Planning – Refers to a child's ability to carry out a verbal or written direction with ease. For example, if you ask a child to touch their head, the child would have to think about lifting their hand and then placing it on their head. The child "planned" the motor action. There are many fun activities that help children increase their motor-planning skills. Here are just a few:
- Play "Follow the Leader," "Simon Says," or sing movement songs such as "The Hokey Pokey," or "The Bunny Hop."
- Begin with giving one direction at a time and then increase the number of directions as the children's skill levels progress.
- Ask the children to repeat the directions before performing the actions. This is extremely helpful for many children.

Body Awareness – Body awareness refers to a child's ability to understand where their body is in space. Children who lack body awareness can appear clumsy, awkward, or even accident prone. People need to understand where their bodies are in space in order to sit down on chairs, pick up objects, run, or open and close jars, boxes, and drawers. Children who need help developing body awareness need many activities that help teach them to know where their body is in space. Any activity that involves pushing, pulling, lifting, dragging, riding, or carrying can be of assistance. There is nothing better than a playground: swinging, sliding, climbing on a jungle gym, or hanging from the monkey bars is extremely beneficial for developing body awareness.

Bilateral Integration – Is the ability to use both sides of the body together, such as coordinating two hands together and using them in conjunction with one another without difficulty or delay. When a child catches a ball, the child is coordinating how both hands will be used. When a child strings beads, one hand is holding the string and the other hand is placing the bead on the string. The body is learning how to work together. Jumping activities, clapping games, playing musical instruments, beading, lacing, and pouring activities can also help develop bilateral integration.

Crossing Midline – Is the ability to bring the upper extremities across the body to perform the desired actions. The midline refers to the center line of the body, extending from the head to the toe. When we cross our legs, one leg has crossed the midline. Here are some activities to facilitate crossing the midline.
- Encourage the children to reach across the body for materials with each hand.
- The establishment of hand dominance is still developing in early childhood. Never discourage a child from using the right or left hand. Encourage the natural development of hand dominance by placing objects or presenting materials at midline, and then allow the child to freely choose which hand is used.
- When painting at an easel or drawing on the chalkboard, encourage the child to create a continuous line across the entire page on the easel or on the chalkboard.
- Play games which help children identify their right and left sides. Have them kick balls or play movement games that focus on both sides of the body.

Fine Motor Skills
A Developmental Checklist ✔

✔

Between Ages of Two and Three:

- ☐ Imitates circular scribble and horizontal and vertical lines
- ☐ Builds a tower of 6 blocks
- ☐ Holds crayon with thumb and fingers *(not fist)*
- ☐ Snips with scissors
- ☐ Puts tiny objects in small containers
- ☐ Folds paper in half
- ☐ Pulls toys with strings
- ☐ Strings 1 to 4 large beads
- ☐ Uses a spoon
- ☐ Turns single pages of a book
- ☐ One hand begins to be dominant
- ☐ Paints with some wrist action
- ☐ Pounds, rolls, pulls, and squeezes play dough

Between Ages of Three and Four:

- ☐ Builds a tower of 9 blocks
- ☐ Snips with scissors
- ☐ Completes a 5–6 piece puzzle
- ☐ Holds a crayon with three fingers
- ☐ Copies a circle
- ☐ Copies vertical and horizontal lines
- ☐ Draws a person with a head
- ☐ Uses a spoon and fork with little spillage
- ☐ Opens rotating door handles
- ☐ Strings ½ inch beads
- ☐ Traces a square
- ☐ Unzips separating zipper; zips and unzips non-separating zipper
- ☐ Unbuttons large and small buttons
- ☐ Identifies body parts

Between Ages of Four and Five:

- ☐ Builds a tower of 10 blocks
- ☐ Strings ¼ inch beads
- ☐ Scissor skills improved – cuts on lines and cuts simple shapes
- ☐ Copies a cross and a square

- ☐ Can independently button and unbutton
- ☐ Laces shoes
- ☐ Uses dominant hand with better coordination
- ☐ Able to do 6–10 piece puzzles
- ☐ Can print some uppercase letters
- ☐ Draws a person with 2 to 4 body parts
- ☐ Holds writing tools with three fingers – control increasing
- ☐ Dresses and undresses independently – managing buttons and zippers
- ☐ No longer switches hands in the middle of an activity
- ☐ Builds a 6 block pyramid

Between Ages of Five and Six:

- ☐ Bounces and catches balls
- ☐ Builds a tower of 12 blocks
- ☐ Can build 3 steps from 6 blocks
- ☐ Draws angles, triangles, and other geometric shapes
- ☐ Draws a complete person with a head, body, legs, arms, and a face
- ☐ Can color within lines
- ☐ Cutting skills improved - can cut along lines and can cut out a circle
- ☐ Holds a knife in the dominant hand
- ☐ Copies first name
- ☐ Has mastered an adult grasp of a pencil
- ☐ Hand dominance is well-established
- ☐ Can use paste and glue appropriately
- ☐ Prints numerals 1 to 5
- ☐ Enjoys working with a variety of mediums: paint, clay, glitter, chalk, glue, etc.
- ☐ Begins to tie shoes
- ☐ Can "sew" lacing cards
- ☐ Completes a 12–15 piece puzzle
- ☐ Learning how to print upper- and lowercase letters

Getting Ready
Strengthening Hands, Wrists, and Fingers

Play Dough

Play dough is always fun for young children to play with, and it is an excellent tool to help build and develop hand strength as well as manual dexterity. The following simple activities will be enjoyed by the children and they will help them to further develop their fine motor skills.

- Pretend you are baking cookies. Flatten the dough with a rolling pin and use cookie cutters to create shapes. Plastic lids, plastic cups, and plastic silverware may be used for cutting and making shapes with the play dough.

- Roll the play dough in long thin snake shapes. Cut the play dough snakes with scissors.

- Use a variety of kitchen tools. Play dough can be squeezed through a potato ricer, garlic press, or pushed through a funnel. Plastic forks, spoons, and knives can be used to cut play dough and to create impressions in the play dough.

- Place two small balls of play dough, each a different color, in a small plastic bag. Push and squeeze the play dough until it is one color. For example, squeezing a yellow ball of play dough with a blue ball of play dough will create green play dough.

- Children love making their own play dough. The following recipes have been tried and tested in classrooms and have been found to be incredibly successful.

Great Play Clay
You will need: I cup cornstarch, 2 cups baking soda, 1 ¼ cups water, liquid tempera paint or food coloring, mixing bowl, and a microwave-safe bowl.

What you do: Mix the cornstarch and baking soda together in a mixing bowl. In a microwave-safe bowl, mix the water with the paint or food coloring. Slowly add the flour mixture to the water and stir. Microwave the mixture for several minutes, stopping to stir every 30 to 40 seconds, or cook on the stove over a low heat for approximately 15 to 20 minutes while stirring constantly. When air-dried this play dough will harden and can then be painted.

No-Cook Baker's Clay

You will need: 4 cups flour, 1 cup salt, 1 teaspoon powered alum, 2 cups water, and food coloring.

Special Tip: For even distribution of color, add the food coloring to the water before the water is mixed with the other ingredients.

What you do: Mix the flour, salt, and powdered alum together. Slowly mix the water into the flour mixture and then knead for several minutes. Divide the dough into smaller balls and then add a different food coloring to each section of dough. Store in airtight containers. Use cookie cutters or create your own shapes. Place on an ungreased cookie sheet and bake for 30 minutes in an oven set at 250°. Turn the dough over and bake another 30 minutes.

Fluffy Snow Play Dough

You will need: 1 cup Ivory Snow Flakes™ detergent, 3 cups warm water, mixing bowl, and an electric mixer.

What you do: First add the food coloring to the water. Then add the soap flakes and beat with an electric mixer until the soap is fluffy and can be manipulated. If you want to pretend that this is "real" snow, leave out the food coloring and simply make "snow white" play dough.

No-Cook Super Sand Play Dough

You will need: 4 cups of clean play sand, 3 cups flour, 1 cup water, and ¼ cup vegetable oil.

What you do: Combine the flour, sand, water, and oil in a mixing bowl. Knead with your hands until the mixture forms a ball. If the mixture is too dry, gradually add water until it reaches a nice dough consistency. If the mixture is too watery, gradually add more flour. This is a super play dough for children who really enjoy tactile experiences.

Edible Oatmeal Play Dough

You will need: 2 cups creamy peanut butter, 2 cups rolled oats or oatmeal, 2 cups powdered milk, ²/₃ cup honey, food coloring, mixing bowl, and a spoon or utensil for stirring.

What you do: Mix all the ingredients together in a large bowl. After washing your hands, stir and knead until the mixture feels like play dough. This dough is great fun to play with. It is "edible," but it is recommended only in very small samples.

Glitter Play Dough

You will need: I cup flour, I cup water, ½ cup salt, I tablespoon vegetable oil, 2 teaspoons cream of tartar, food coloring, a saucepan, a spoon or utensil for stirring, and glitter.

What you do: Mix all the ingredients together in a saucepan over a medium-low heat. Keep stirring until the dough forms a ball. Remove the dough from the pan and cool. Add glitter to the dough and knead until smooth. This is one play dough recipe that should NOT be refrigerated. Stored in an air-tight container, this play dough will last for several weeks at room temperature.

Special Tip: Add vanilla extract to any homemade play dough recipe and it will help prevent mold, preserve the dough, and smell great!

Juicy Fruit Play Dough

You will need: 2 cups flour, I cup salt, I cup boiling water, 2 tablespoons vegetable oil, 4 tablespoons cream of tartar, 3 ounce package of sugar-free gelatin, a saucepan, and a spoon or utensil for stirring.

What you do: Mix all of the ingredients together in a mixing bowl. Bring the water and oil to a boil and then pour in the other ingredients. Turn the heat to low and stir the ingredients until the mixture forms a ball. Pour onto a piece of waxed paper to cool. Once the play dough is cool, enjoy playing with the great-smelling play dough!

"Goopy" Recipes

These are two "goopy" recipes that children will love to touch and feel. The sensation of molding, stretching, and squishing the goopy stuff is so much fun! Even as an adult you might find yourself wanting to play with "the goop."

Rubbery Goop

You will need: 2 cups baking soda, I ½ cups water, and I cup cornstarch.

What you do: Place all the ingredients in a saucepan over medium heat and stir until smooth. This mixture needs to boil and be stirred constantly until it is thick. Remove from the heat and cool. Now let the children enjoy the feel and texture, as well as the movement, of this rubbery goop!

Slimy Goop

You will need: ½ cup white glue, food coloring *(optional)*, ¼ cup liquid starch, and a wooden spoon.

What you do: Put all the ingredients in a bowl and mix with a wooden spoon, craft stick, or tongue depressor. Let the children get their fingers sticky and have a lot of "goopy" fun!

Pouring and Scooping Activities

Children's explorations with pouring and scooping activities will help build a variety of skills. By sifting sand or pouring water, children improve their manual dexterity as well as their eye-hand coordination. They also enhance their cognitive skills as they discover many properties of the various materials or by observing such principles as cause and effect. Not only do pouring and scooping activities improve fine motor and other skills, but children delight with the opportunity to play with sand and water materials.

Big Bucket Fun

If you do not have a water table, fill big buckets or tubs with water. Give the children soap chips, measuring spoons and cups, plastic bottles, butter tubs, and sponges to play with in the water. Put towels or newspaper on the floor so the children will not slip on the wet floor. When children play with water and sand, give them toys like eggbeaters, watering cans, and squeeze bottles.

Cotton Ball Scoop

Filling a large bowl full of cotton balls can provide children with a wonderful pretend snow experience. Give the children spoons and have them scoop out cotton balls, one at a time. How many can they scoop in 10 seconds? 30 seconds? This also makes for a fun relay race.

Extra Fun: Soap Bubbles

Add ½ cup of liquid dish soap to 2 quarts of water. Have the children blow bubbles with small plastic containers (frozen juice) open at both ends. They can also blow bubbles by using straws or green plastic berry baskets. Also let the children wash dishes in the soapy water.

Containers and Diggers

- bowls
- buckets
- shovels
- ladles
- spoons
- scoops
- cups
- pans

Sifters

- colander
- funnel
- rake
- sieve
- sifter
- strainer

Natural Materials

- seeds
- shells
- sticks
- pebbles and rocks
- sand
- dried peas
- dried beans
- uncooked rice
- foam packing material
- salt
- uncooked oatmeal

Tossing and Turning Activities

Tossing and turning activities can help develop wrist strength and increase eye-hand coordination. The following activities will assist in building these fine motor skills.

Large Mat Beanbag Shape Game

You will need a discarded plastic window shade, a vinyl tablecloth, or a plastic shower curtain. With a permanent black marker, draw a 12-square grid with a shape in each square. Color each shape a different color.

Give the children beanbags to toss onto the grid. They must tell you the name of the shape and its color. You can also play the game by telling the children which shape to aim for, and watch if they can toss the beanbag onto the shape that you have specified.

Hot Potato

Play "hot potato" using a real potato. Have the children sit in a circle. Play some music and have the children toss the potato around the circle quickly. When the music stops, the person holding the potato gets to be the next person to start and stop the music.

Hopscotch Games

You will need a discarded plastic window shade, a vinyl tablecloth, or a plastic shower curtain. Cut the plastic into strips that can be taped together to make a long indoor sidewalk. Divide the sidewalk into squares or prepare as a hopscotch grid.

Draw different things in each of the squares, such as shapes, colors, animals, or alphabet letters. The children can toss beanbags onto the sidewalk and then name the thing that appears on the square where the beanbag has landed.

Flip and Catch

You will need plastic spatulas and tissue paper. The children will play in pairs. One child places the tissue paper on the spatula and then flips it to their partner. The partner tries to catch the tissue paper and flip it back to the other child.

Pancake Restaurant

Make pretend pancakes from thick cotton batting. Let the children use a real frying pan and spatulas. They can pretend they are making pancakes and flip and turn them in the pan.

Clown Beanbag

Find a cardboard box. Draw a big clown face on the box and then cut out the eyes, nose, and mouth. Children delight in trying to throw beanbags through the facial features.

Printing and Stamping Activities

Printing and stamping activities are fun for children and they will strengthen their hand, wrist, and finger muscles and increase their coordination skills.

Build a Classroom Stamp Collection

Scrapbooking and the craft of stamping have become popular hobbies. Ask the parents of your students to donate stamps that they may no longer be using. You will be surprised with how many stamps you receive.

Food Stamps

Apples and potatoes make great tools for stamping and printing. Draw a shape on the food and then carve around the shape so it is raised. Dip it in the tempera paint and then press and print on paper. Marshmallows, carrots *(with the end cut)*, and cucumbers *(cut in half)* make great stamps for dabbing pictures made out of circles—similar to the art of pointillism.

Make Your Own Stamps

Save old wooden blocks. Cut out shapes, letters, or numbers *(in reverse)* from craft foam, self-adhesive shoe liners, or heavy self-adhesive mounting tape. Craft foam will have to be glued to the surface of a wooden block. Peal the paper off the backing paper from the self-adhesive mounting tape and shoe liners and simply stick the foam to the wooden block.

This is an inexpensive way to create stamps for young children. Wooden blocks are easy for small hands to hold and control. Use commercially purchased stamping ink or tempera paint poured in tin pie pans.

Nature Printing

You will need: tempera paint, pie tins, paper, and various objects from nature, such as vegetables and fruit cut in half and leaves.

What you do: Pour tempera paint into the pan. Pour in just enough paint to cover the bottom of the pan. Lay an object, such as a leaf, in the paint and then gently press it onto the paper.

Sponge Prints

You will need: Sponges cut into small squares, pie pans, liquid tempera paint, paper, and clothespins. *(The sponges can be cut into many different shapes.)*

What you do: Fill the pie pans with a variety of paint colors. Attach a clothespin to each sponge. The clothespin serves as a handle for the sponge and makes it easier for the child to manipulate. Let the children dab paint on the paper. Point out how mixing two colors can create a new color.

Extra ideas: Instead of a sponge, try using a shower scrunchy for a different texture. Look for other materials that would be fun to use with paint.

Finger Plays and Puppet Activities

The use of finger plays and finger puppets are effective tools for helping children learn how to control finger movement, increase coordination, and enhance manual dexterity. Children have to listen, watch, and learn how to correctly make the finger movements that go with each of the sentences in a finger play.

It is helpful if you first have the children learn specific names for each finger: thumb, pointer, tall finger, ring finger, and pinkie. (You may choose your own names.) Knowing individual names for each finger can assist children in better understanding oral directions.

Photographic Finger Puppets

Using a digital camera and a word processor makes it possible to create unique and personal finger puppets. After taking a photograph, cut the face out of the photo and glue it to a strip of construction paper that can be taped around a finger tip.

Film Container Finger Puppets

You will need: film containers, wiggle eyes, felt, glue, and other craft objects of your choice.

What you do: Film containers are easy to balance on finger tips. Turn the containers upside down and then add eyes and other facial features. Create film container puppets according to the characters needed for the finger play you have chosen.

Finger Puppet Garden Gloves

Use inexpensive garden gloves to create a finger puppet glove. Attach or draw faces on each finger tip. A great idea is to draw Red Riding Hood, the Wolf, the Woodcutter, Grandmother, and Red Riding Hood's Mother on each of the glove's fingertips. The children can then hold up the correct character as they listen to the story about Little Red Riding Hood.

Another fun idea is to make the Three Billy Goats Gruff and the Troll as well as the Three Pigs and the Wolf. It will be worth your time to make classroom gloves to be used as you tell these traditional stories.

Garden Glove Individual Fingertip Puppets

To make individual finger puppets, simply cut off the fingers from a garden glove. Decorate each finger with buttons, beads, pom-poms or by drawing on facial features with thin permanent markers.

Finger Plays

Pat-a-Cake

Pat-a-cake, pat-a-cake, baker's man!
Bake me a cake as fast as you can.
Pat it and dot it, and mark it with a B,
And put it in the oven
For baby and me.
        –Mother Goose

*This rhyme is also fun to do with a partner.
Clap your own hands together and then clap the
hands of your partner. Do this in rhythm to the
rhyme.*

(Clap four times in rhythm)
(Cup hands.)
(Pantomime this action.)
(Extend both hands.)
(Point to a classmate and then point to yourself.)

Open, Shut Them

Open, shut them; open, shut them;
Give a little clap.
Open, shut them; open, shut them;
Lay them in your lap.

Creep them, creep them slowly upward
To your rosy cheeks.
Open wide your shiny eyes
And through your fingers peep.

Open, shut them; open, shut them;
To your shoulders fly
Like them, like little birdies,
Flutter to the sky.

Falling, falling, slowly falling,
Nearly to the ground.
Quickly raising all your fingers,
Twirling them around.

Open, shut them; open, shut them;
Give a little clap.
Open, shut them; open, shut them;
Lay them in your lap.
        –Traditional

Fun with Hands

Roll, roll, roll your hands as slowly as can be;
Roll, roll, roll your hands;
Do it now with me.

Roll, roll, roll your hands as slowly as can be;
Roll, roll, roll your hands;
Do it now with me.

Continue the rhyme by substituting these phrases:
Clap, clap, clap your hands.
Shake, shake, shake your hands.
Stamp, stamp, stamp your hands.
Tap, tap, tap your fingers.

Here's a Cup of Tea

Here's a cup, and here's a cup,
    *(Make a fist with the left hand and
    then with the right hand.)*
And here's a pot of tea;
    *(Add a spout to the right hand by
    protruding the thumb.)*
Pour a cup, and pour a cup,
    (Pour into the left hand and then into the right.)
And have a cup with me!
    *(Extend cup to neighbor and
    pretend to be drinking.)*

Finger Game

This belongs to father;	*(Hold up thumb.)*
This belongs to mother;	*(Hold up pointer finger.)*
This belongs to sister;	*(Hold up the middle finger.)*
This belongs to brother;	*(Hold up the ring finger.)*
And this belongs, if you would know,	
To grandfather; we love him so.	*(Hold up little finger.)*

Then a little bird, you understand,	
Builds a nest in the palm of your hand;	*(Cup hand.)*
And then the birdies fly away;	*(Flutter fingers)*
We'll follow to see where they stay.	*(Make fingers go up the opposite arm.)*
Follow, follow, follow, follow;	
Here they are up in the hollow!	*(Place fist under the opposite arm.)*

Eency Weency Spider

The eency weency spider	
Went up the water spout;	*(Fingers imitate a moving spider.)*
Down came the rain and	*(Fingers imitate falling rain.)*
Washed the spider out;	
Out came the sun and	*(Arms make a large circle.)*
Dried up all the rain.	
And the eency weency spider	
Went up the spout again.	*(Fingers imitate a moving spider.)*

Two Little Houses

Two little houses closed up tight.	*(Two fists closed.)*
Open the windows and let in the light.	*(Spread hands apart.)*
Ten little people stand tall and straight.	*(Hold up ten fingers.)*
Ready for the bus at half past eight.	*(Fingers make running motion.)*

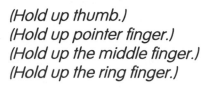

Where is Thumbkin?

Where is thumbkin?	*(Hide both hands behind your back.)*
Where is thumbkin?	
Here I am.	*(Bring the right hand from behind your back and wiggle the thumb.)*
Here I am.	*(Bring the left hand from behind your back and wiggle the thumb as if "talking" to the right thumb.)*
Very nice to see you.	*(Wiggle right thumb.)*
Very nice indeed sir.	*(Wiggle left thumb.)*
Run away.	*(Hide right hand behind your back.)*
Run away.	*(Hide left hand behind your back.)*

(Repeat using pointer finger, middle finger, ring finger, and pinkie in place of thumbkin.)

Little Miss Muffet

Little Miss Muffet,	*(Make fist with thumb erect.)*
Sat on a tuffet,	
Eating her curds and whey.	*(Pretend to eat.)*
Along came a spider,	*(Make running motions with fingers.)*
And sat down beside her,	*(Move fingers toward Miss Muffet.)*
And frightened Miss Muffet away.	*(Show palms of hands.)*

–Mother Goose

That's Me!

This is me,	*(Point to self.)*
I'd like you to meet.	*(Bow.)*
I have one little head,	*(Shake head.)*
And two little feet.	*(Shake feet.)*
I have two little arms,	*(Hold up arms.)*
And one little nose.	*(Touch nose.)*
And ten little fingers,	*(Wiggle fingers.)*
And ten little toes.	*(Wiggle toes.)*

Swinging Birds

Two tall telephone poles,
> *(Hold up hands, palms inward, pointer fingers out.)*

Across them a wire is strung.
> *(Extend middle fingers until they touch at tips.)*

Two little birds hopped on,
> *(Move thumbs to touch extended middle fingers.)*

And swung and swung and swung.
> *(Swing hands back and forth.)*

Counting

1, 2, 3, 4, 5,
> *(Clap five times)*

I caught a fish alive.
> *(Loud clap.)*

6, 7, 8, 9, 10,
> *(Clap five times)*

I let it go again.
> *(Show palms of hands.)*

Here is a Bunny

Here is a bunny with ears so funny.
> *(Two fingers up straight.)*

Here is the hole in the ground.
> *(Make circle with fingers.)*

Up go his ears and he runs to his hole,
> *(Motion of running fingers.)*

When he hears a strange little sound.
> *(Clap hands.)*

Five Little Speckled Frogs

Five little speckled frogs sitting on a speckled log,
    (Hold up five fingers.)
Eating some most delicious bugs, yum, yum.
    (Rub your tummy.)
One jumped into the pool, where it was nice and cool,
    (One finger pretends to jump into a pool.)
Then there were four speckled frogs, glub, glub.
    (Everyone says, "glub, glub.")

Four little speckled frogs sitting on a speckled log,
    (Hold up four fingers.)
Eating some most delicious bugs, yum, yum.
    (Rub your tummy.)
One jumped into the pool, where it was nice and cool,
    (One finger pretends to jump into a pool.)
Then there were three speckled frogs, glub, glub.
    (Everyone says, "glub, glub.")

Three little speckled frogs sitting on a speckled log,
    (Hold up three fingers.)
Eating some most delicious bugs, yum, yum.
    (Rub your tummy.)
One jumped into the pool, where it was nice and cool,
    (One finger pretends to jump into a pool.)
Then there were two speckled frogs, glub, glub.
    (Everyone says, "glub, glub.")

Two little speckled frogs sitting on a speckled log,
    (Hold up two fingers.)
Eating some most delicious bugs, yum, yum.
    (Rub your tummy.)
One jumped into the pool, where it was nice and cool,
    (One finger pretends to jump into a pool.)
Then there was one speckled frog, glub, glub.
    (Everyone says, "glub, glub.")

One little speckled frog sitting on a speckled log,
    (Hold up one finger.)
Eating some most delicious bugs, yum, yum.
    (Rub your tummy.)
He jumped into the pool, where it was nice and cool,
    (One finger pretends to jump into a pool.)
Then there were no speckled frogs, glub, glub.
    (Everyone says, "glub, glub.")

(Use as a finger play or let the children make their own set of stick puppets. Reproduce the patterns so each child has a copy. The children color the patterns, cut them out, and tape them so they fit around their fingertips. Most young children will need assistance with cutting out the patterns. The children can remove a frog finger puppet at the end of each verse.)

This Little Cow

This little cow eats grass.
> *(Hold up one finger.)*

This little cow eats hay.
> *(Hold up a second finger.)*

This little cow drinks water,
> *(Hold up a third finger.)*

And this little cow runs away.
> *(Hold up a fourth finger.)*

This little cow does nothing
But lie and sleep all day.
> *(Hold up a fifth finger.)*

(Use as a finger play or let the children make their own set of stick puppets. Reproduce the patterns so each child has a copy. The children color the patterns, cut them out, and tape them to craft sticks or tongue depressors. Most young children will need assistance with cutting out the patterns.)

Five Little Squirrels

Five little squirrels sat up in a tree.
(Hold up five fingers.)
The first squirrel said, "What do you see?"
(Wiggle the thumb.)
The second squirrel said, "I see a bee."
(Wiggle the pointer finger.)
The third squirrel said, "Don't sting me."
(Wiggle the middle finger.)
The fourth squirrel said, "Let's all run."
(Wiggle the ring finger.)
The fifth squirrel said, "This is not fun."
(Wiggle the pinkie finger.)
And away the squirrels ran, every one!
(Wiggle all the fingers.)

(Use as a finger play or let the children make their own set of stick puppets. Reproduce the patterns so each child has a copy. The children color the patterns, cut them out, and tape them so they fit around the child's finger tips. Most young children will need assistance with cutting out the patterns. The children can remove all the squirrel finger puppets on the last verse.)

Here's a Little Washboard

Here's a little washboard;
> *(Two hands together with
>   fingers pointed down.)*

Here's a little tub;
> *(Make circle with arms.)*

Here's a little cake of soap;
> *(Make a circle with two hands.)*

And here's the way we scrub.
> *(Make rubbing motions.)*

Here's a line way up high;
> *(Middle fingers touching.)*

Now the clothes are drying;
> *(Hold palms up.)*

Here the wind comes whistling by;
> *(Wave arms.)*

See! The clothes are flying.
> *(Make swinging motions with arms.)*

(Use as a finger play or let the children make their own set of stick puppets. Reproduce the patterns so each child has a copy. The children color the patterns, cut them out, and tape them to craft sticks or tongue depressors. Most young children will need assistance with cutting out the patterns. The children say the rhyme and hold up the appropriate pattern for each verse.)

SOAP

SOAP

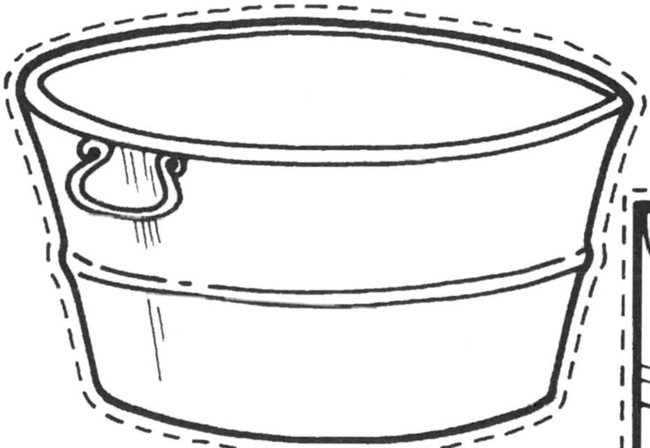

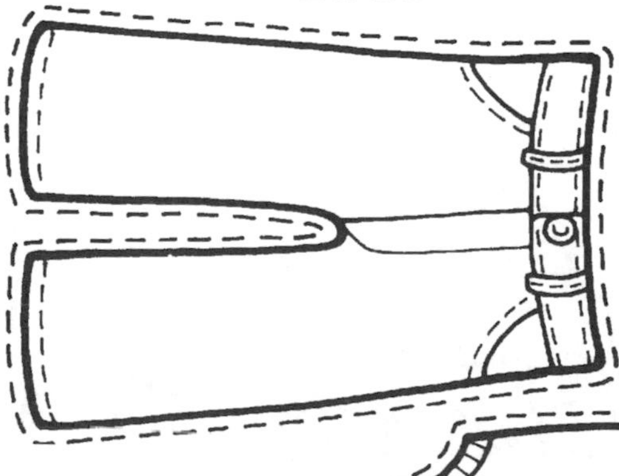

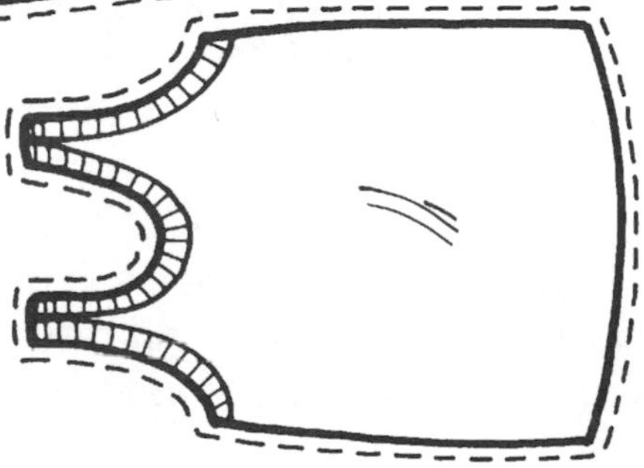

WASH

Squeezing and Tweezing Activities

Spray bottles, tweezers, glue bottles, hole punches, empty plastic bottles, *(i.e. ketchup and mustard bottles),* and clothespins are wonderful tools for increasing finger strength and fine motor skills.

Tweezing Seed Pictures

The children will need construction paper, black markers, glue, and a variety of large seeds. The best seeds for this activity can be found in pumpkins and large squash. Wash and dry the seeds.

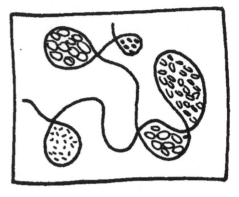

Ask the children to draw a scribble design with a black marker on a piece of construction paper. Fill each section with glue (squeeze) and have the children use a tweezer to place the seeds on the glue. The seed designs are attractive and it is a great exercise for developing fine motor skills.

Squeezing Puffy Paint

You will need: flour, salt, liquid tempera paint, card stock or cardboard, empty squeeze bottles *(with narrow nozzles),* mixing bowls, and paper towels.

What you do: Mix equal parts of flour, salt, and water together in a bowl. Add tempera paint for color. Mix well and pour into a squeeze bottle that has a narrow nozzle. Squeeze the puffy paint onto cardboard or heavy stock paper. The mixture will become hard when it dries.

Make Your Own Colored (or Glittered) Glue

You will need: old markers, water, mixing bowl, and small bottles of white glue

What you do: Do not throw away those old markers! Place them in a bowl of water and let them soak until you see the water starting to turn color. Place the soaked markers in separate bottles of glue and let them soak overnight. By the next day you will have bottles of colored glue. The children can use the glue just like a puff paint.

The children can squeeze the bottle and create designs on a piece of paper. The children will have fun tracing over the smooth glue lines with their fingers when the art is dry.

Extra ideas: Add glitter to the colored glue for an extra fun effect and added texture. You can also use the colored glue to write names, letters, and numbers. Trace with fingertips.

Paper Plate Magic

You will need: Water-based color makers, heavy paper plates, and a spray bottle with water.

What you do: Give each child a paper plate and let them color all over it with water-based markers. When the children have finished their drawings, have them take turns using the spray bottle, and give their drawings a "spray." The colors will blend together and the plates will look beautiful. It is so much fun to watch the colors as they blend together.

Fun with Tweezers

You will need: A tweezer, a muffin tin, and a bowl filled with interesting small items, such as colored paper clips, buttons, small pom-poms, acorns, erasers, rubber bands, gold fish crackers, bean seeds, craft jewels, or whatever else you find handy.

Directions: Give the child the bowl of objects, the muffin tin, and the tweezers. Have the child pick up the items using the tweezers and then sort the objects by placing them into the individual muffin tin sections. Children enjoy this activity and it will increase their finger strength and manual dexterity.

Eye-Dropper Art

You will need: Paper, an ice cube tray, eyedroppers, and coffee filters.

What you do: Cover the workspace with newspaper. Flatten a dry circular coffee filter and lay it on the newspaper. Fill the sections of an ice cube tray with water. Add several drops of food coloring to each section of the ice cube tray. Using eyedroppers, drop the colored water on the coffee filter. The more color you add, the more the colors will spread and blend.

Wonderful Wet Coffee Filters

You will need: Water-based color markers, coffee filters, and a spray bottle filled with water.

What you do: Flatten a coffee filter and spray with water until it is fairly wet. Using water-based markers, draw on the filter. The colors will blend and spread.

Paper Hole Punch

Using a paper hole punch is a excellent way to build strength in the hand, wrist, and finger muscles. Copy the patterns on page 24 onto card stock. Let the children have fun using a hole punch to punch out the holes where indicated on the patterns.

Make Fresh-Squeezed Orange Juice or Lemonade

Buy oranges and/or lemons for the children in your classroom to make fresh-squeezed orange juice or lemonade. The children will improve their fine motor skills and they will delight in making and drinking this tasty-treat!

Reproducible Cards to Hole Punch

Directions are on page 23.

Clothespin Activities

Pinching clothespins onto a bucket or clothesline are excellent activities for strengthening fingers and hands. These activities will also increase coordination skills. Pinching a clothespin together to create open and close movements is done by moving and coordinating the thumb and pointer finger. Clothespins are also wonderful tools to use in creating a multitude of creative fine motor and academic games.

Classroom Clothesline

Set up a clothesline in your room and have a basket of clothes with a box of clothespins nearby. The children can use these during creative play time and hang up the clothes to dry. The children will have fun playing and will be building their fine motor skills.

Matching T-Shirts/Clothes/Socks

Play matching games using the patterns found on the following pages: T-shirt patterns on page 27, clothing patterns on page 28, and sock patterns on page 29.

Make multiple copies of each of the pages, making sure that each page is printed on a different colored card stock. Cut out the patterns and place them by the clothesline with a box of clothespins. The children can hang up the items on the clothesline by matching them according to color or by the design on the item.

Cotton Ball Race

Divide the class into two teams. Each team has one clothespin, a bowl of cotton balls, and an empty bowl. The goal is to pick up the cotton balls, one at a time, with a clothespin and place them in the empty bowl. The first team to move all the cotton balls from one bowl to the other bowl is the winning team.

Colored Clothespins

You will need an assortment of sizes and colors of clothespins. If you cannot locate colored clothespins, you can paint wooden clothespins.

Place the colored clothespins in a learning center along with pattern cards. The children can create the pattern printed on the card by placing the clothespins along the top of a bucket or on the side of a paper plate in the same order as seen on the card.

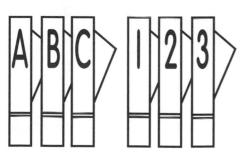

Clipping Letters and Numbers

Put a string up like a clothesline. Write alphabet letters or numerals on wooden clothespins. The students can clip the letters onto the clothesline in alphabetical sequence or they can match uppercase and lowercase letters. They can also clip the clothespins in numerical sequence. Older children might try to spell their names or other words on the clothesline.

Clothespin Games

Specific Directions for the Clothespin Wheel Games

The reproducible patterns for three different clothespin wheel games can be found on pages 30–32. Construction for each of the clothespin wheel games is the same. Reproduce the game page of your choice. Color the large circle according to specific directions, cut it out, and glue it onto a sturdy paper plate or a cardboard circle. Cut out the small squares and glue them to the tops of the clothespins. All the games involve matching the small image on the clothespin to the corresponding larger image on the circle. Clip the clothespin by the correct image on the circle.

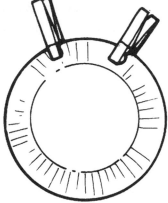

Clothespin Wheel: Mother and Baby Animals

Color all of the mother animals and each of the baby animals. Let the children enjoy clipping each clothespin baby to its correct mother.

Clothespin Wheel: Colors

Color each circle as indicated. Let the children enjoy clipping each colored clothespin to the matching color on the color wheel.

Clothespin Wheel: Numbers One to Ten

No additional coloring is necessary for this game. Let the children enjoy clipping each numeral clothespin to the matching numeral on the wheel.

Specific Directions for the Clothespin Cans

The reproducible patterns for three different clothespin can games can be found on pages 33–35. Construction for each of the clothespin can games is the same. Reproduce the game page of your choice. Color according to the specific directions, cut it out, and glue the two long strips (8 squares) along the top of a can or bucket. Cut out the small squares and glue them to the tops of the clothespins. All the games involve matching the small image on the clothespin to the corresponding larger image on the can. Clip each clothespin by the correct image on the can.

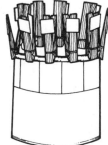

Clothespin Can: Rhyming Pictures

Color each of the pictures. Let the children enjoy matching the pictures that rhyme by clipping the smaller picture to the rhyming larger picture.

Clothespin Can: Numerals, Sets, and Number Words

No additional coloring is necessary. The children will clip the matching numeral and number word clothespin to the correct sets of dots on the can. Two clothespins can be attached to each set of dots.

Clothespin Can: Sight Words

Color each of the pictures. The children will read and attach the clothespin word to the matching picture on the can.

T-Shirt Patterns

Complete directions are found on page 25.

✂ 27 ✂

Clothing Patterns

Complete directions are found on page 25.

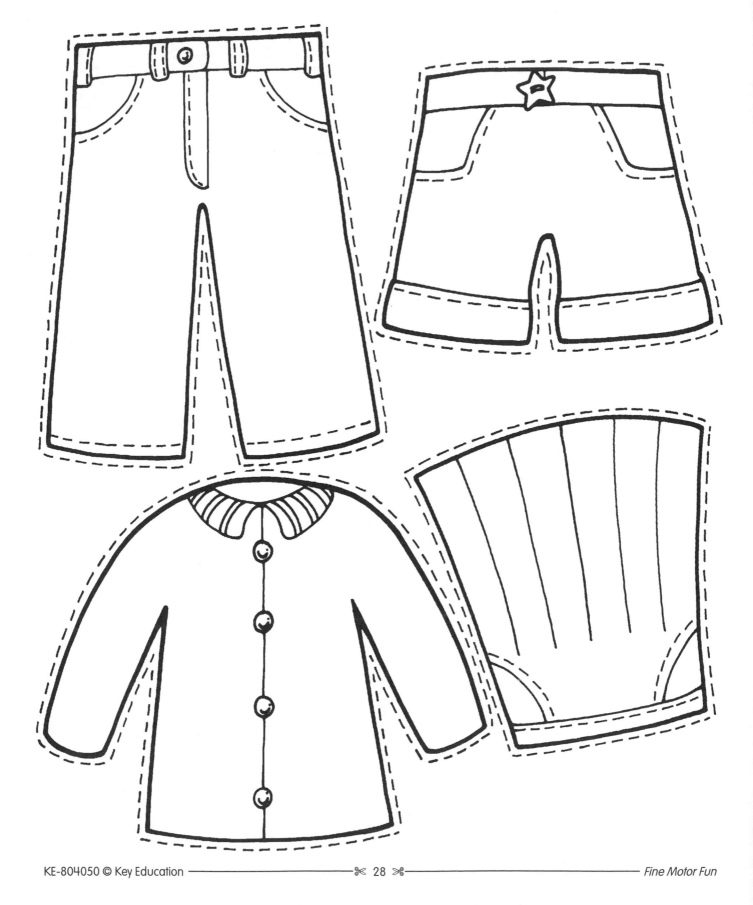

Sock Patterns

Complete directions are found on page 25.

Clothespin Wheel:
Mother and Baby Animals

Complete directions are found on page 26.

(Color each animal. Cut out
the large circle and
glue it onto the center
of a paper plate.)

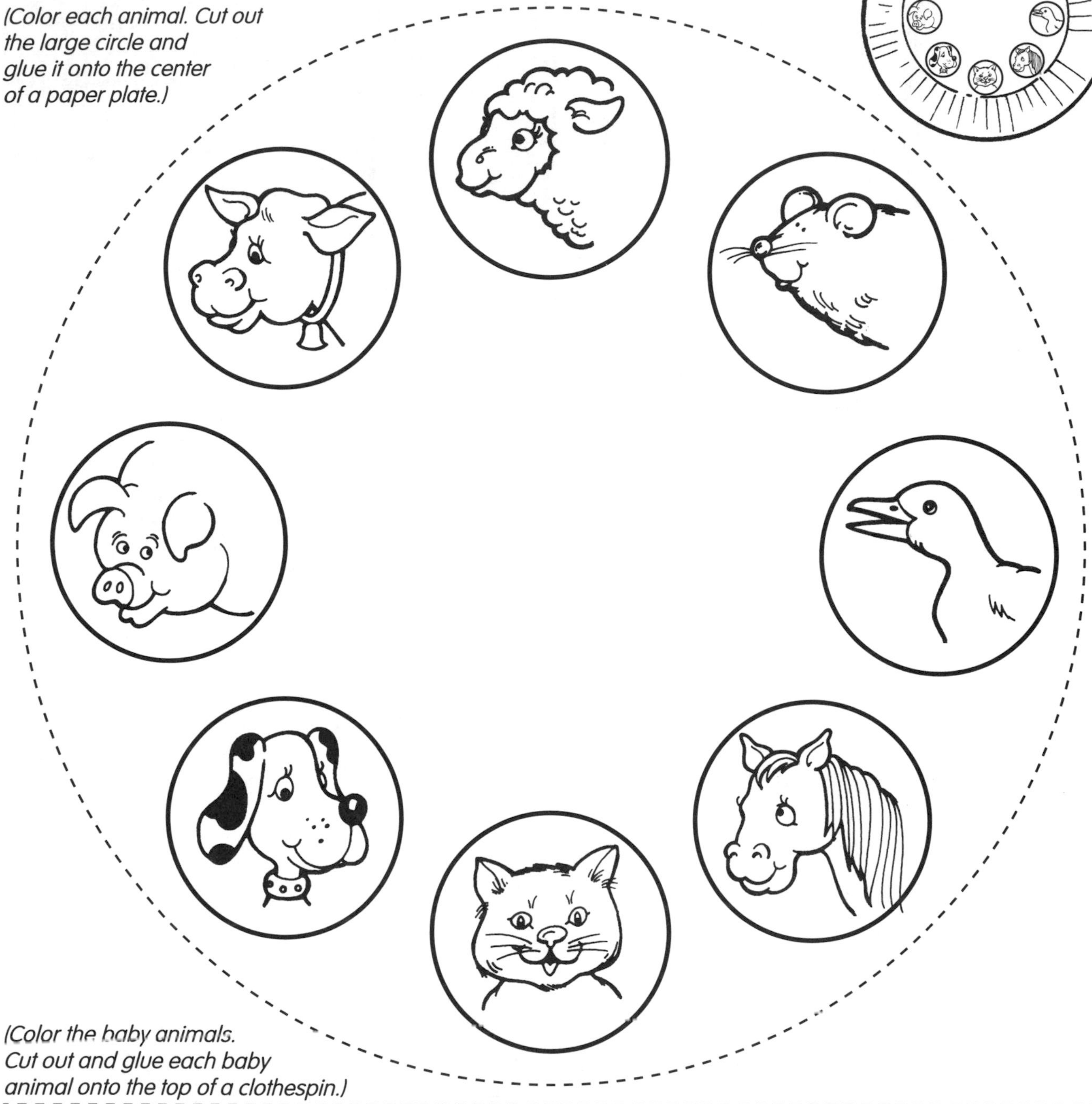

(Color the baby animals.
Cut out and glue each baby
animal onto the top of a clothespin.)

Clothespin Wheel: Colors

Complete directions are found on page 26.

(Color each circle as indicated. Cut out the large circle and glue it onto the center of a paper plate.)

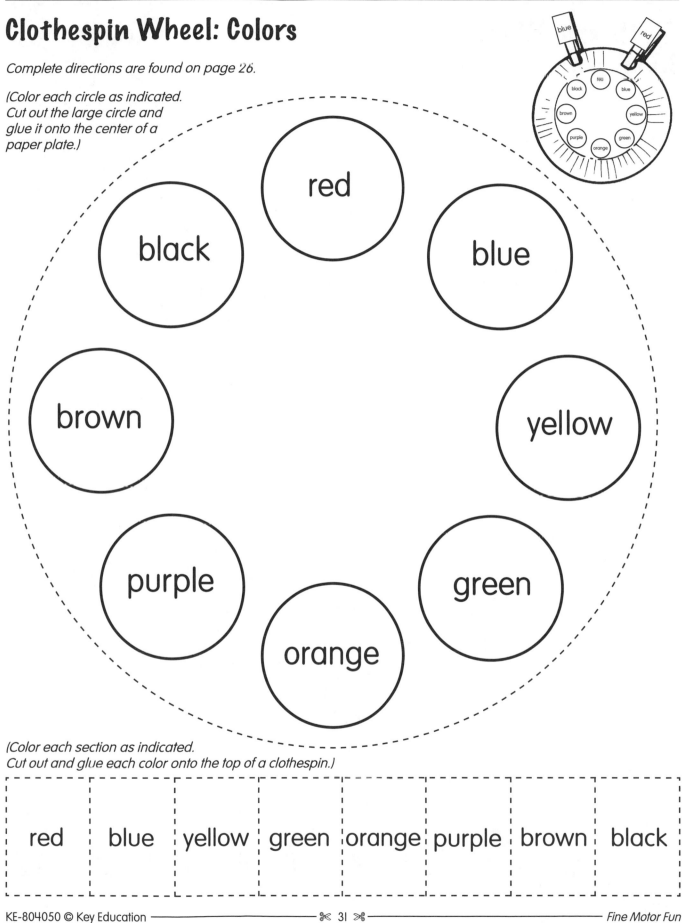

red

black

blue

brown

yellow

purple

green

orange

*(Color each section as indicated.
Cut out and glue each color onto the top of a clothespin.)*

red	blue	yellow	green	orange	purple	brown	black

Clothespin Wheel:
Numbers One to Ten

Complete directions are found on page 26.

*(Cut out the circle
and glue it onto the center
of a paper plate.)*

*(Cut out and glue each
numeral onto the top of a clothespin.)*

Clothespin Can:
Rhyming Pictures

Complete directions are found on page 26.

(Cut out and glue each picture onto the top of a clothespin.)

(Color, cut out, and glue to the top of a can or bucket.)

Clothespin Can: Numerals, Sets and Number Words

Complete directions are found on page 26.

(Cut out and glue each numeral or number word onto the top of a clothespin.)

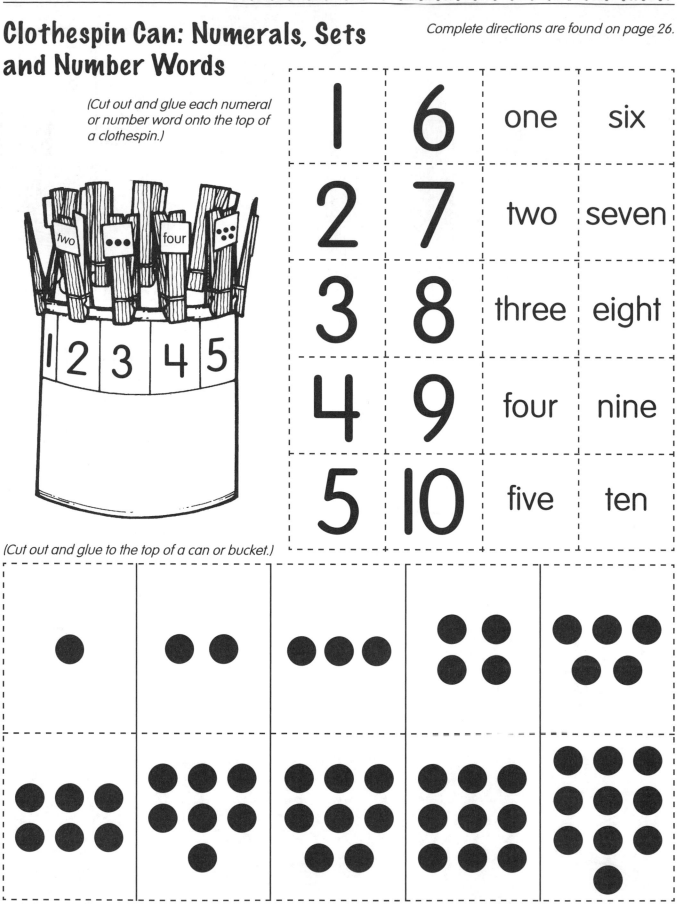

1	6	one	six
2	7	two	seven
3	8	three	eight
4	9	four	nine
5	10	five	ten

(Cut out and glue to the top of a can or bucket.)

Clothespin Can:
Sight Words

Complete directions are found on page 26.

(Cut out and glue each word onto the top of a clothespin.)

cat	dog
pig	boy
girl	car
sit	run
man	bed

(Color, cut out, and glue to the top of a can or bucket.)

Gluing and Sticker Fun

Puffy Glue

Mix equal parts of shaving cream with glue. You can add food coloring for color if you want. Use a craft stick to stir and to put on the paper. The mixture will puff up when it dries

Great Glue for Kids

You will need: 3 tablespoons cornstarch, 4 tablespoons cold water, 2 cups boiling water, and a squeeze-type container.

What you do: Mix the cornstarch and cold water in a small bowl and then pour the mixture into the boiling water, stirring constantly. When the liquid is clear and thick, remove from the heat and let cool. Pour into a plastic squeeze container and label properly. Children will love the experience of making their own glue.

Colored Rice and Pasta Noodles

You will need: A variety of uncooked pasta noodles or rice, 2 teaspoons food coloring, 3 teaspoons rubbing alcohol, a container with an air-tight lid, and waxed paper.

What you do: Mix the food coloring and the rubbing alcohol in the container. Place the pasta or rice in the container and cover. Then shake the container so the color is evenly distributed on the rice and pasta. Spread the colored rice or pasta onto waxed paper and allow to dry. It will take several hours for the pasta to dry completely. The colored rice or pasta can be glued on paper, pots, or wood. The colored rice can also be used like glitter. Using a paintbrush, spread glue on a piece of paper and have the children drop the rice onto the glue. The pasta noodles will also be used in the lacing and stringing section *(page 37)*.

3-D Tissue Paper Pictures

Cut a variety of colors of tissue paper into small squares. Take a piece of tissue paper and wrap it around the eraser end of a pencil. Dip the tissue paper into a small container of glue and then press it onto a piece of paper. The tissue will be standing on the paper and look like a flower. Create abstract designs, fill in coloring book pages with the 3-D tissue paper, or make your own 3-D picture designs.

Sticker Ideas

Stickers can provide children with hours of fun and help improve their fine motor skills. Create rebus sticker stories; draw a bus and fill it with people and animal stickers; create a farm scene and add farm animal stickers; on black construction paper create a space picture with outer space and alien stickers; or use blue construction paper to create an ocean or underwater scene with fish stickers.

Paper Chains

Children can make long paper chains by gluing together the ends of 6" x 1" construction paper strips. Glue sticks work very well for this activity.

Lacing and Stringing Fun

Building fine motor skills and increasing eye-hand coordination is fun for young children when they participate in playing with lacing and stringing activities.

Reproducible Lacing Card Patterns

Lacing cards are enjoyed by both boys and girls. Use the patterns provided on pages 38–42. Copy the patterns onto heavy card stock or trace onto cardboard. Color the pictures, laminate for durability, and then punch out the holes where indicated. The children can lace the cards using real shoelaces, curling ribbon, or yarn. Wrap masking tape around one end of the yarn to create a "needle."

Reproducible Stringing Patterns

Use the patterns provided on pages 43–46. Copy the patterns onto colored card stock, cut out, laminate for durability, and then punch out the holes where indicated. The children can string the objects using real shoelaces, curling ribbon, or yarn. Wrap masking tape around one end of the yarn to create a "needle."

Home-Made Lacing Cards

Pictures from discarded coloring books, toy catalogs, discarded children's books, or greeting cards can make inexpensive lacing cards. Simply glue the pictures onto heavy card stock or cardboard, cover with self-stick laminate, punch holes, and the cards will be ready to lace.

Colorful Pasta Noodles

Colored rice and pasta can be wonderful materials for use in a multitude of lacing and stringing activities. Use the recipe for colored rice and pasta noodles found on page 36.

Rice: The colored rice can be used like glitter. Using a paintbrush, spread glue on paper and have the children drop the rice onto the paper.

Colored Pasta: Colored pasta noodles can provide hours of beading and jewelry-making fun. Color many varieties of pasta noodles and place them in a bucket with some string or yarn. Colored pasta noodles are excellent for beading and patterning activities. Wrap masking tape around the end of the yarn to serve as a needle when stringing pasta noodles.

Jewelry Making

The children will enjoy stringing bracelets and necklaces from a wide variety of materials. Edible necklaces can be made from round cereal and candy. Other kinds of jewelry can be made from small plastic craft beads; buttons; many different kinds of pasta; packing peanuts; drinking straws cut into small pieces; and home-made play dough beads. To make the play dough beads, roll the play dough into balls, poke holes through the middle, and allow to dry.

Beach Ball

Directions: Copy onto card stock, color, and laminate for durability. Punch holes where indicated.
Laces: Wrap masking tape around one end of a piece of yarn (36") to be used as a needle.
Real shoelaces also work well.

Let's Go Fly a Kite

Directions: Copy onto card stock, color, and laminate for durability. Punch holes where indicated.
Laces: Wrap masking tape around one end of a piece of yarn (36") to be used as a needle.
Real shoelaces also work well.

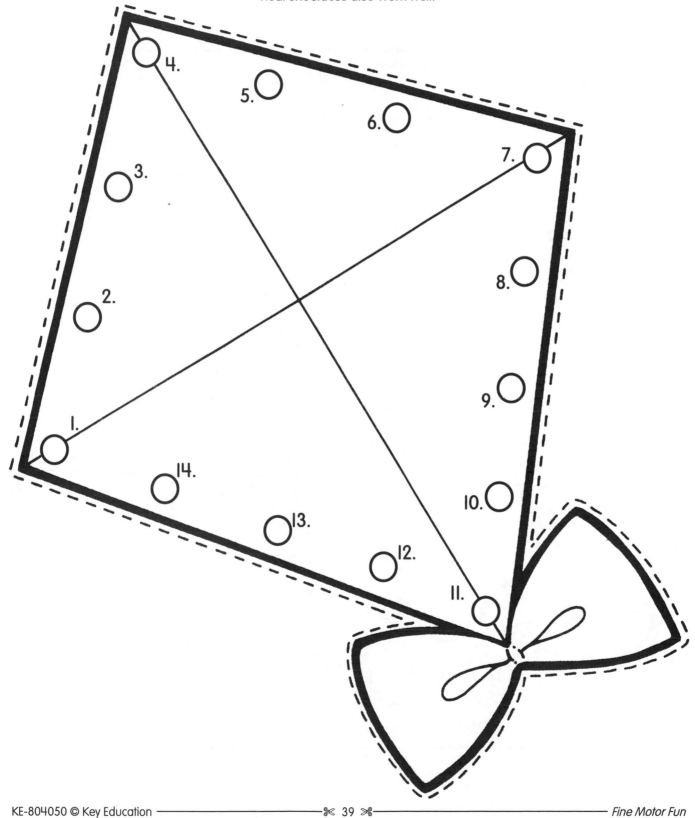

Follow the Road

Directions: Copy onto card stock, color, and laminate for durability. Punch holes where indicated.
Laces: Wrap masking tape around one end of a piece of yarn (36") to be used as a needle.
Real shoelaces also work well.

The Big Frog

Directions: Copy onto card stock, color, and laminate for durability. Punch holes where indicated.
Laces: Wrap masking tape around one end of a piece of yarn (36") to be used as a needle.
Real shoelaces also work well.

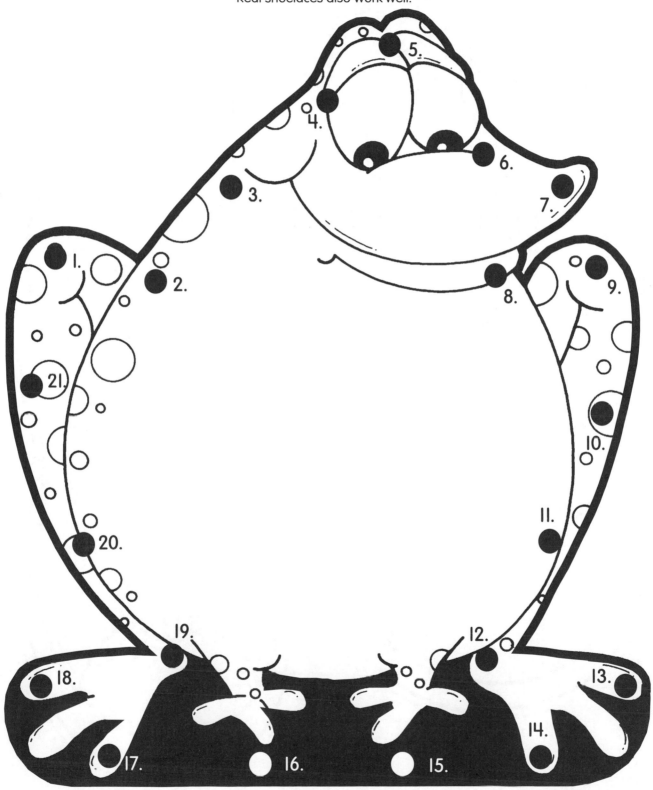

Two Shoes

Directions: Copy onto card stock, color, and laminate for durability. Punch holes where indicated.
Laces: Wrap masking tape around one end of a piece of yarn (36") to be used as a needle.
Real shoelaces also work well.

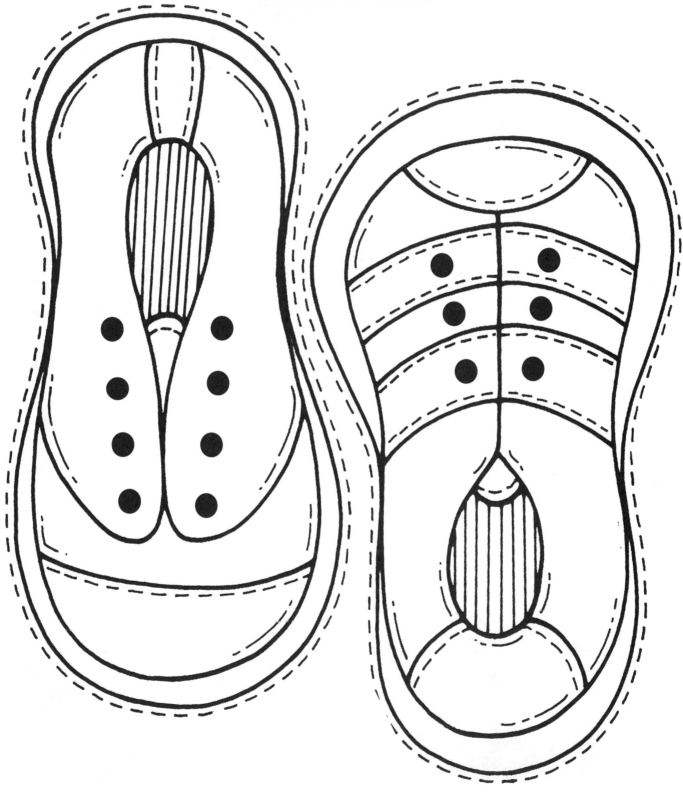

Farm Animal Stringing Patterns

Activity found on page 37.

Directions: Copy onto card stock, color, cut out along the dotted lines, and then laminate for durability. Punch holes where indicated. The children can string the animals together using shoelaces or yarn.

Button Patterns

Activity found on page 37.

Directions: Copy onto colored card stock. Laminate, cut out, and punch two holes in each button. The children can string the buttons together using shoelaces or yarn.

Jewelry Patterns

Activity found on page 37.

Directions: Copy onto colored card stock. Laminate, cut out, and punch a hole in each jewel. The children can string the jewels together using shoelaces or yarn. Adding glitter will makes this jewelry extra fun.

Wooden Bead Patterns

Activity found on page 37.

Directions: Copy onto colored card stock. Laminate, cut out, and punch a hole in each wooden bead. The children can string the beads together using shoelaces or yarn.

Learning to Use Scissors

Early Learning Scissor Activities

Before children can successfully cut with a pair of scissors, they will need to have developed several different skills. First, they must have enough muscle strength to be able to control and coordinate using two hands together *(one hand holds the paper, while the other hand manipulates the scissors)*. They must also be able to isolate the movements of their thumbs, middle fingers, and index fingers. The ability to isolate the action of these fingers allows children to control the opening and closing of the scissors. Here are some helpful suggestions:

- Make sure you have a good pair of scissors that were designed to fit properly in a child's hand.

- Have the children practice touching each finger tip to the thumb. First, touch the pointer finger to the thumb; next the middle finger to the thumb; then the ring finger to the thumb; and finally, the pinkie finger to the thumb.

- Discuss safety prior to giving a child a pair of scissors: You should never run while holding a pair of scissors. You should be sitting when you are cutting with a pair of scissors, and if you are walking with scissors, be sure to hold the blades in the palm of your hand.

- Let the children sit and practice opening and closing the scissors before you give them anything to cut.

- Use a heavier weight paper when first learning how to cut. It is easier to hold and to cut. As the child's skills increase, then introduce lighter weight papers.

- Start with small pieces of paper because they are easier to cut.

- Introduce the concept of "snipping." Let the children snip fringe *(approximately one-inch in length)* on the edge of a strip of paper.

- Let children practice cutting using a wide variety of paper and textures, such as sandpaper, aluminum foil, paint sample squares, wax paper, yarn, straws, play dough, or any other items that you might have handy.

- Be sure that young children have mastered cutting straight lines and geometric shapes before introducing the concept of cutting on a curve.

Snipping Funny Shapes

You will need: scissors, contact paper, and construction paper.

What you do: Let your child enjoy cutting colored construction paper. It does not matter how big or what shapes the pieces are. The adult should cut out and remove the backing on an 8.5" x II" piece of contact paper. When the child has a small pile of colored shapes, she can simply "stick" the shapes on the contact paper. When finished, the contact paper can be turned over and stuck to another sheet of paper. The result is a work of scissor art ready for display.

Scissor Cutting Magazines and Catalogs

You will need: scissors, glue sticks, construction paper, and old magazines and catalogs.

What you do: This simple activity is very educational and is also an activity that children enjoy doing for long periods of time. Simply provide children with the above materials and let them cut out pictures and glue them onto paper using the glue sticks.

This activity can also help children learn how to categorize and sort. Have the children cut out pictures, then sort them into specified categories, such as people, furniture, clothes, or food.

Extra idea: The children will also enjoy making a collage of pictures of their favorite things. Fill a piece of paper or a paper plate with pictures that they have cut out and have them glue them on a piece of paper.

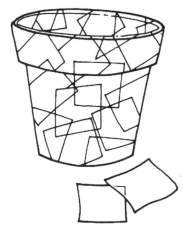

Mosaics

You will need: scissors, white glue, paintbrush, a variety of colored tissue paper, and a clay pot.

What you do: Ask the children to cut many small pieces of colored tissue paper. When they are finished cutting, they can paint the clay pot with diluted white glue. After the pots are covered in glue, the children can place their cut out pieces of tissue paper all over their pots and let them dry.

Extra idea: Provide each child with a simple coloring book page. Have the children use their cut construction paper pieces as mosaics. Using a glue stick, glue the small pieces of paper in each section to finish the page.

The Cutting Box

You will need: scissors, a box, and a wide variety of materials for the children to cut.

What you do: This simple activity will quickly become a classroom favorite. Fill a large box with all sorts of materials that the children can cut. Leave scissors, glue sticks, and paper near the cutting box so the "cut" remnants" can be turned into wonderful art projects. The children will love practicing their cutting skills when they know that they can go to a box where everything in the box is "Okay" to cut!

Rug to Fringe

Directions: Using scissors, snip all the way around the edge of the rug to create fringe.

(The teacher should cut off the edges.)

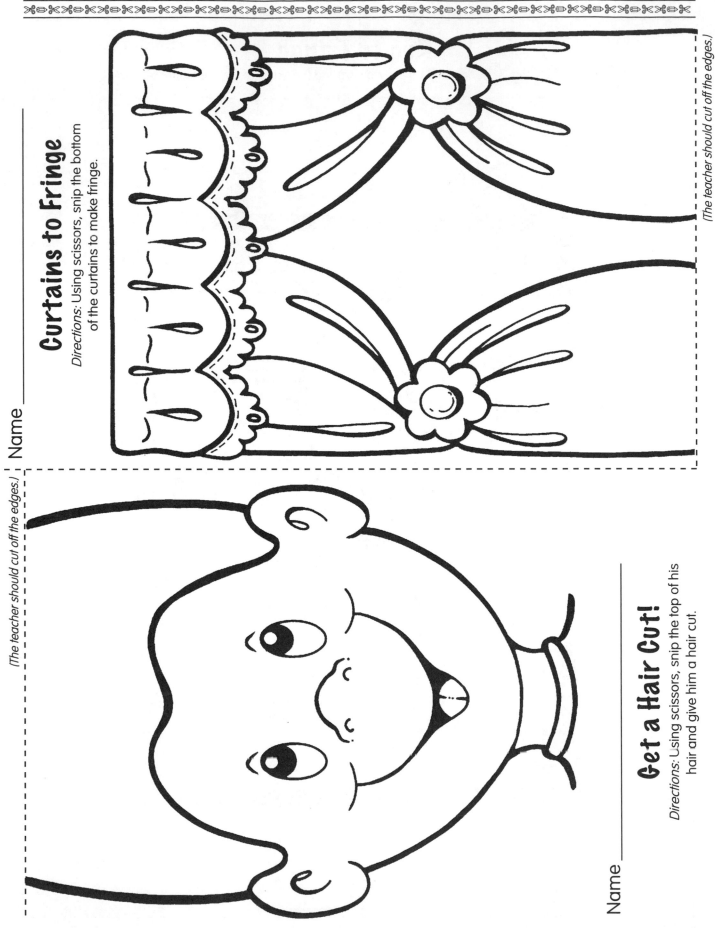

Name _____

Curtains to Fringe

Directions: Using scissors, snip the bottom of the curtains to make fringe.

(The teacher should cut off the edges.)

(The teacher should cut off the edges.)

Get a Hair Cut!

Directions: Using scissors, snip the top of his hair and give him a hair cut.

Name _____

Race Cars

Directions: Help the race cars finish the race. Cut along the straight lines.

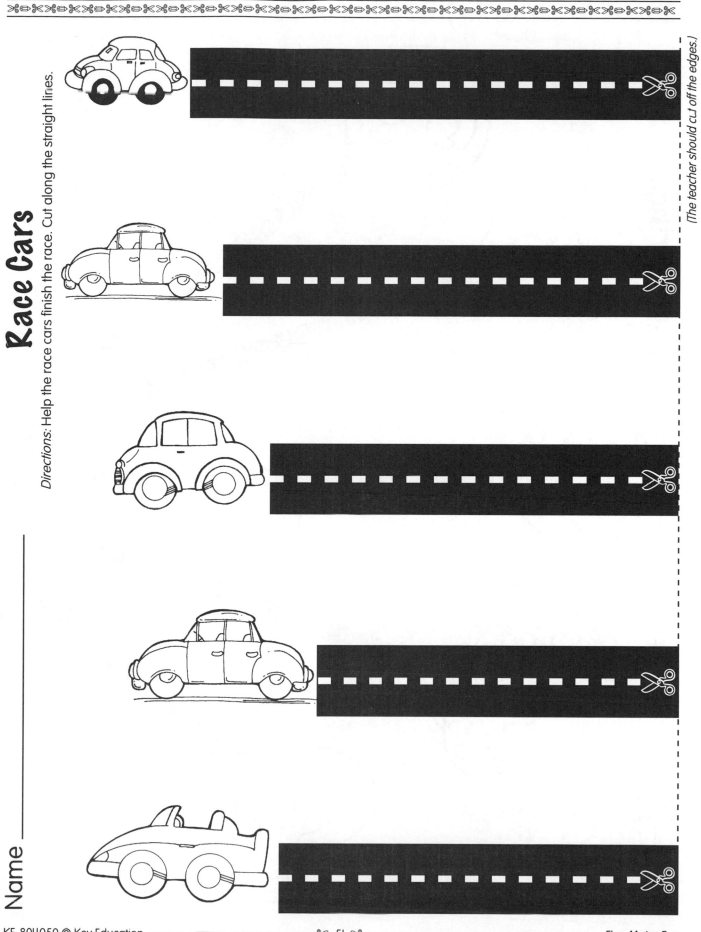

(The teacher should cut off the edges.)

Name _____

Balloon Strings

Directions: Cut along the strings.

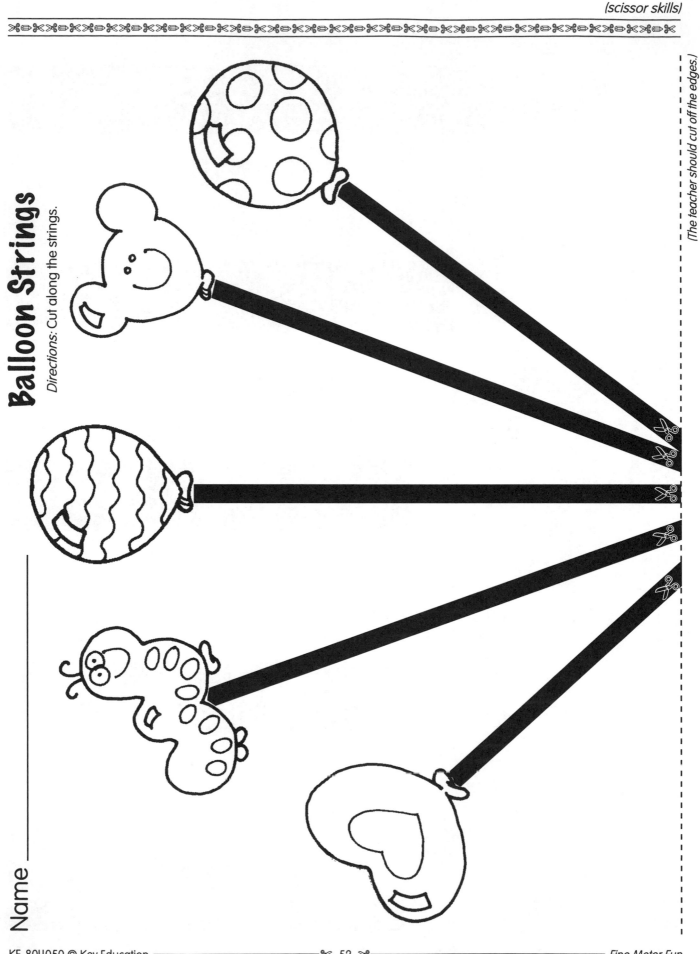

Name

Shooting Star

Directions: Cut along the lines.

(The teacher should cut off the edges.)

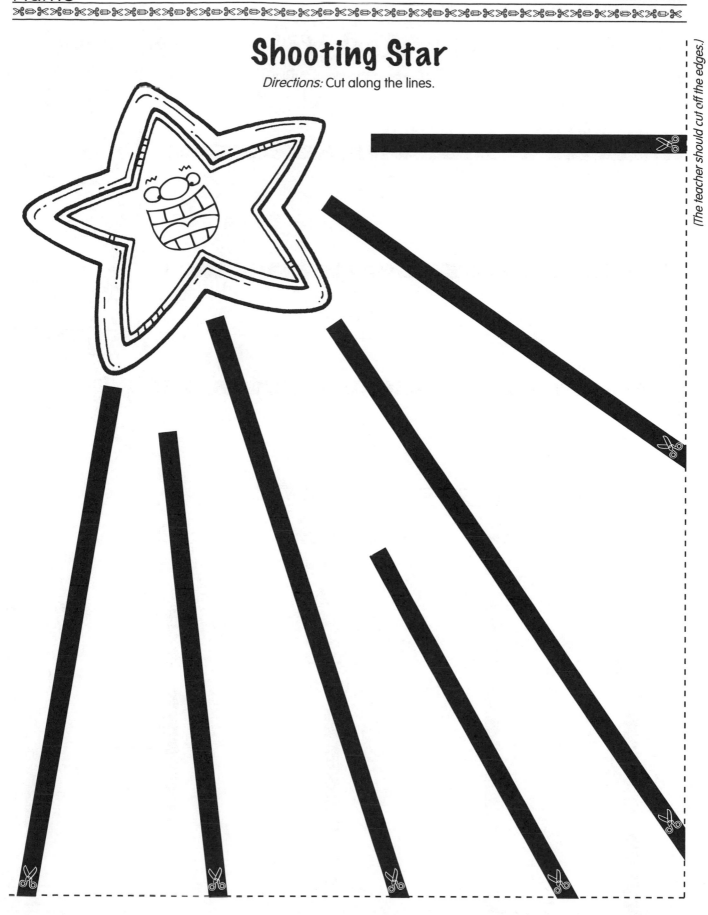

Rockets

(The teacher should cut off the edges.)

Directions: Cut along the lines.

More Rockets

Directions: Cut along the lines.

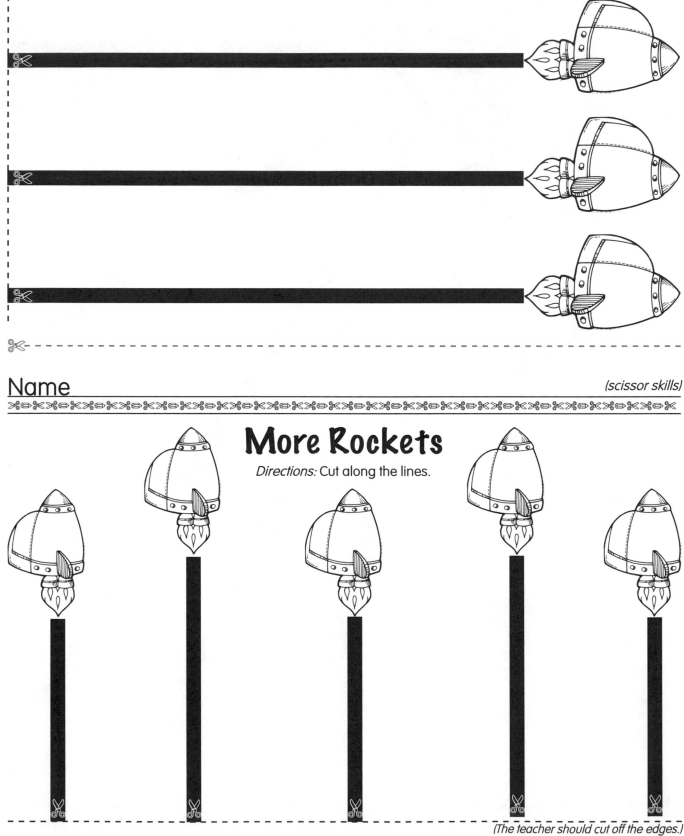

(The teacher should cut off the edges.)

Bugs

Directions: Cut along the lines.

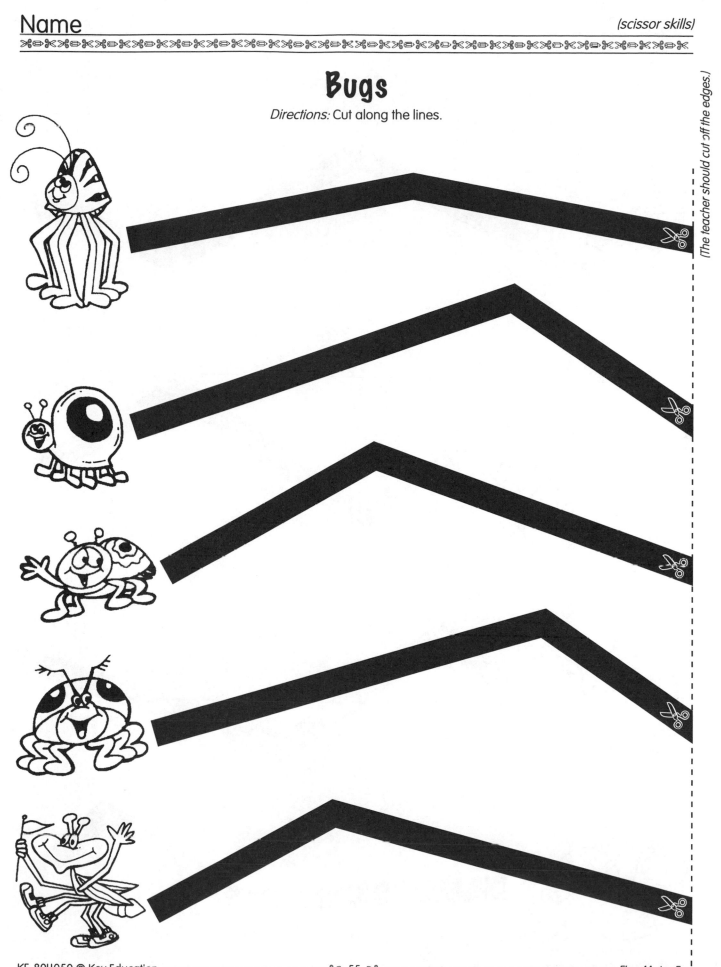

Pets

Directions: Cut along the lines.

(The teacher should cut off the edges.)

Kites

Directions: Cut along the strings.

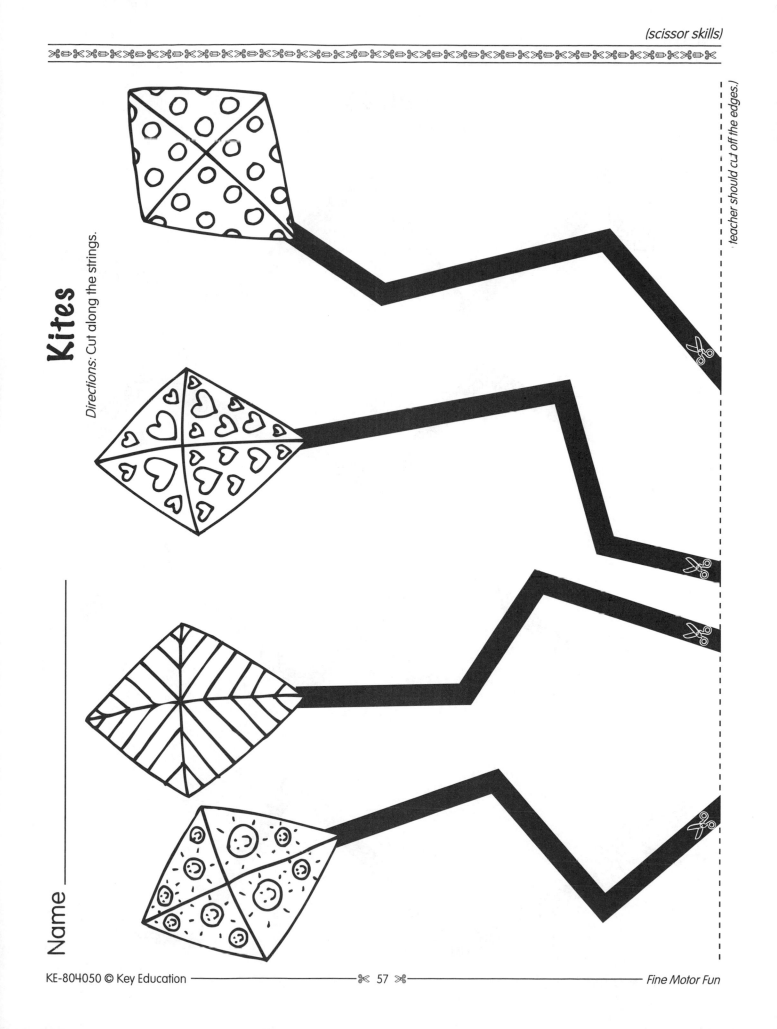

(Teacher should cut off the edges.)

Name _____

Birds

Directions: Cut along the lines.

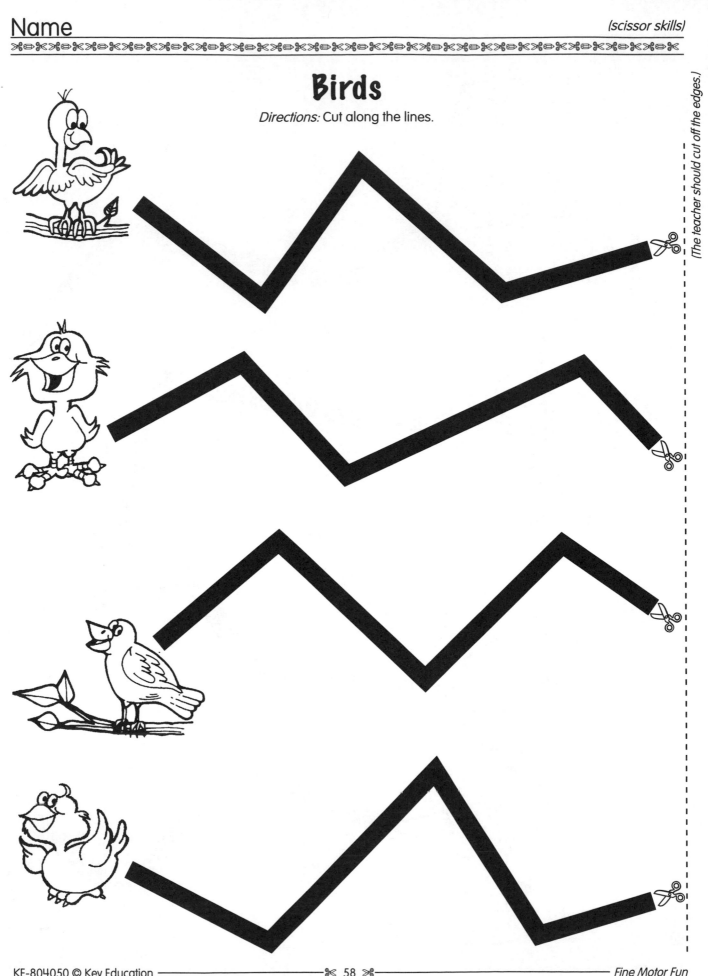

(The teacher should cut off the edges.)

Wild Animals

Directions: Cut along the lines.

Gift Boxes

Directions: Cut out the gift boxes at the bottom of the page. Glue them in the picture.

Mixed-Up Teddy Bear

Directions: Cut out along the solid lines. Arrange the bear and glue him on another sheet of paper.

Funny Fish

Directions: Cut out the fish shapes at the bottom of the page. Glue on the correct spaces.

✂

Doll House

Directions: Cut out the house shapes at the bottom of the page. Glue on the correct spaces.

(scissor skills)

Turtles

Directions: Cut along the lines.

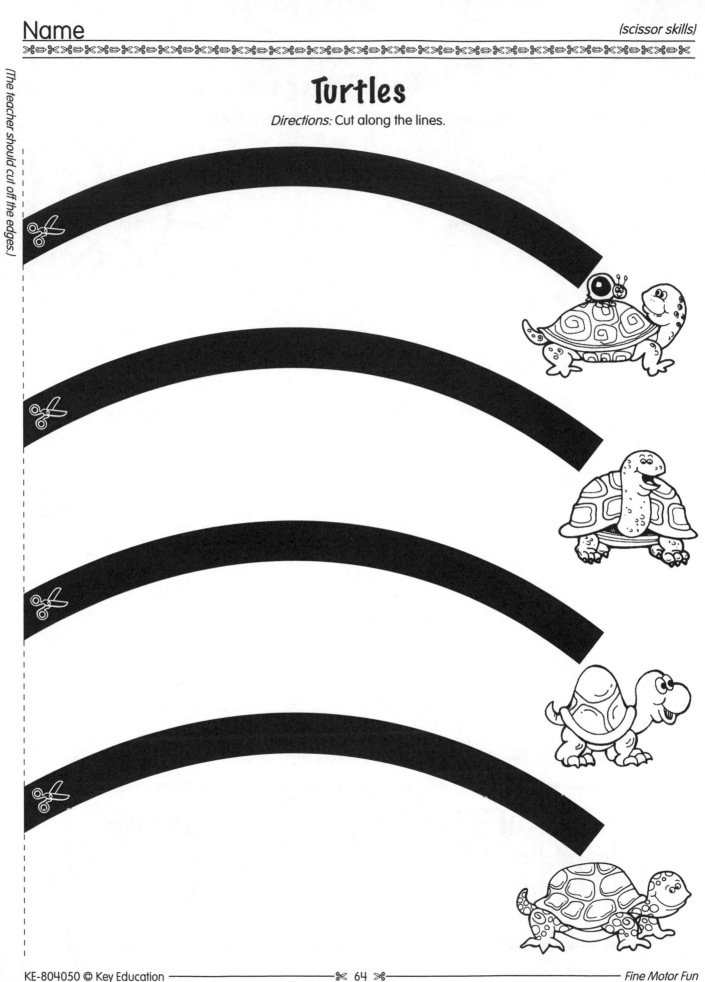

Ants in the Grass

Directions: Cut along the lines.

Name _____

(The teacher should cut off the edges.)

Silly Snakes

Directions: Cut along the lines.

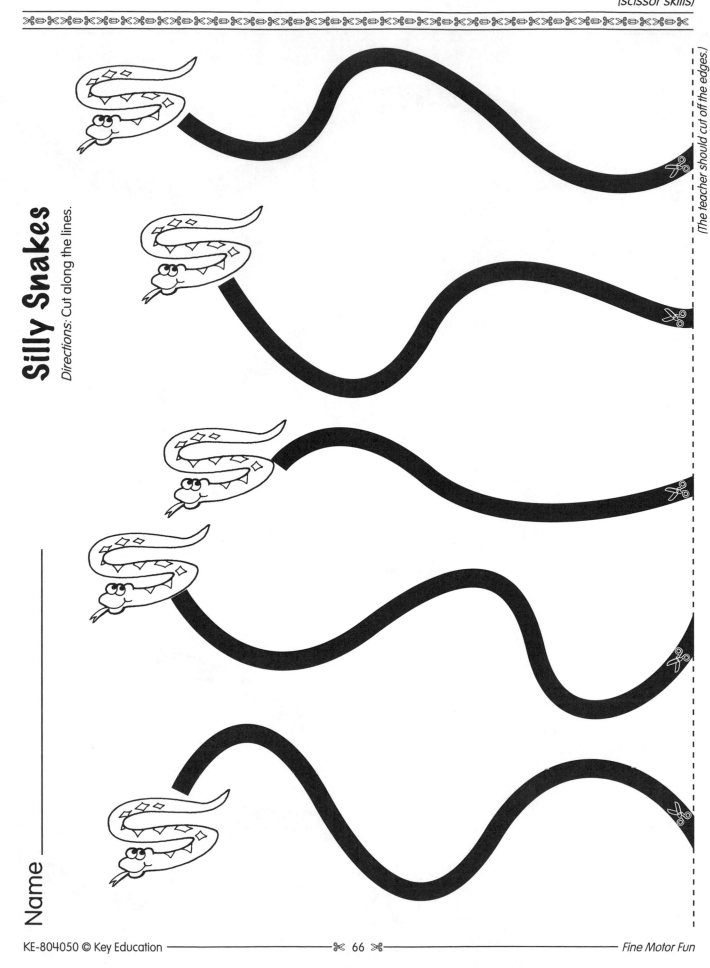

Name

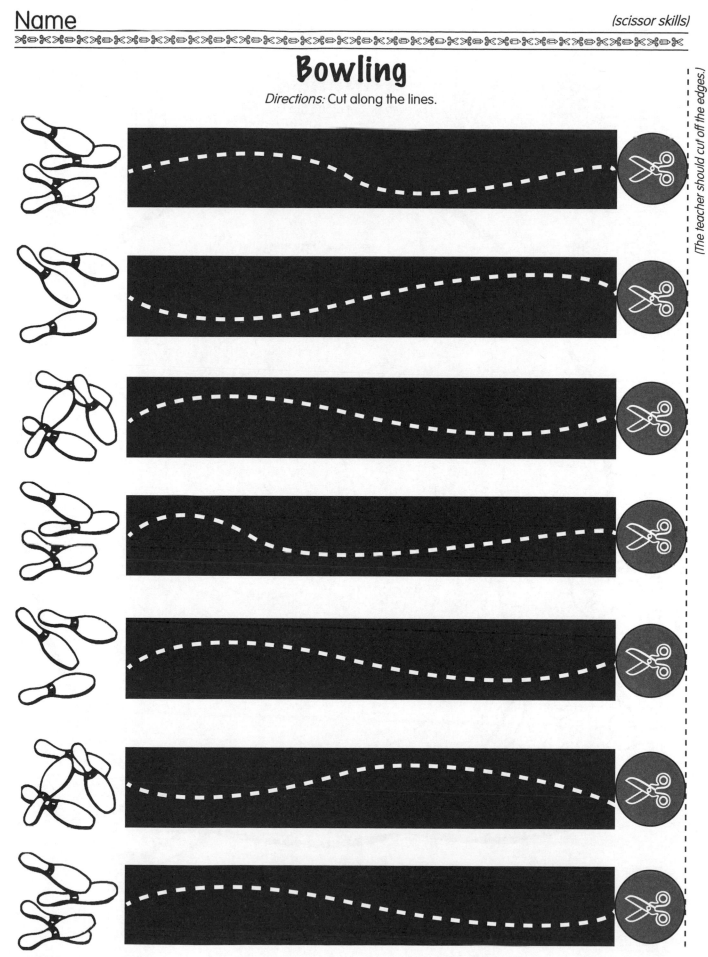

Bowling

Directions: Cut along the lines.

(The teacher should cut off the edges.)

Snail

Directions: Cut along the line.

Cutting Circles

Directions: First cut out the squares. Then cut off the corners to make circles.

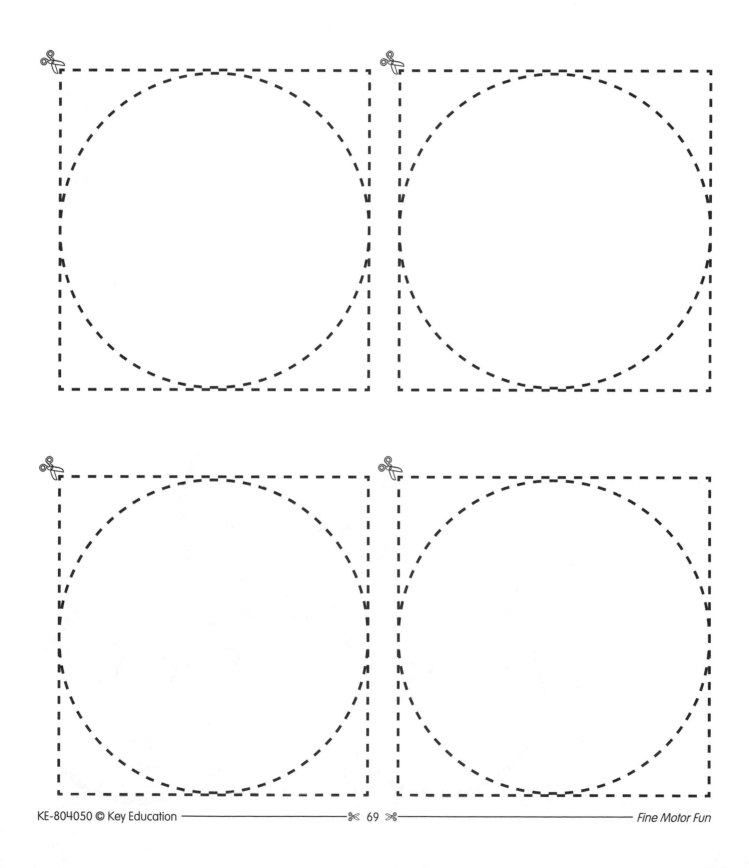

Happy Faces

Directions: Cut out the faces at the bottom of the page. Glue them on the circles.

Scissor Skills Practice

Directions: Begin at the square and cut along the dotted lines. Stop at the circle.

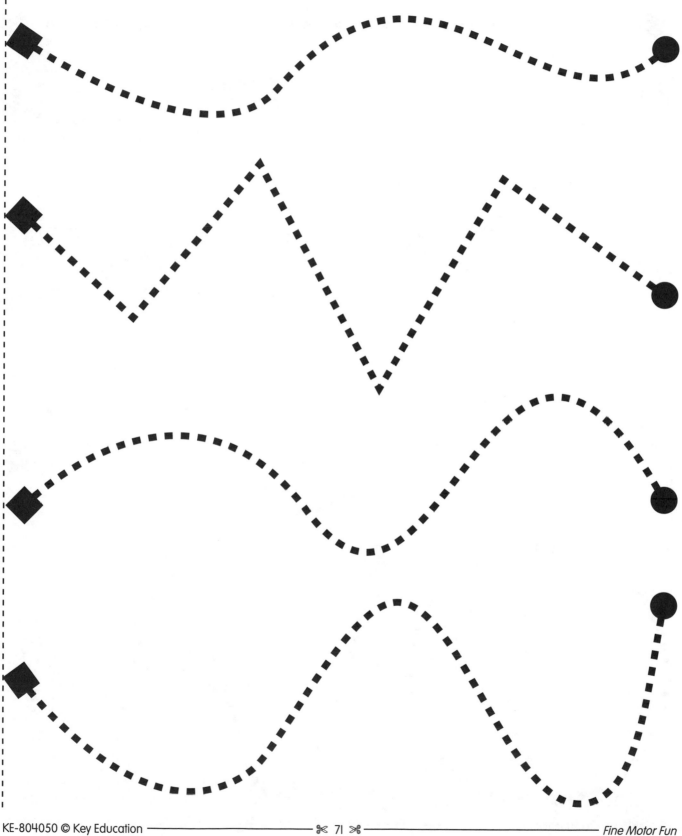

Scissor Skills Evaluation

Directions: Begin at the square and cut along the dotted lines. Stop at the circle.
Cut out the small circle at the bottom of the page.

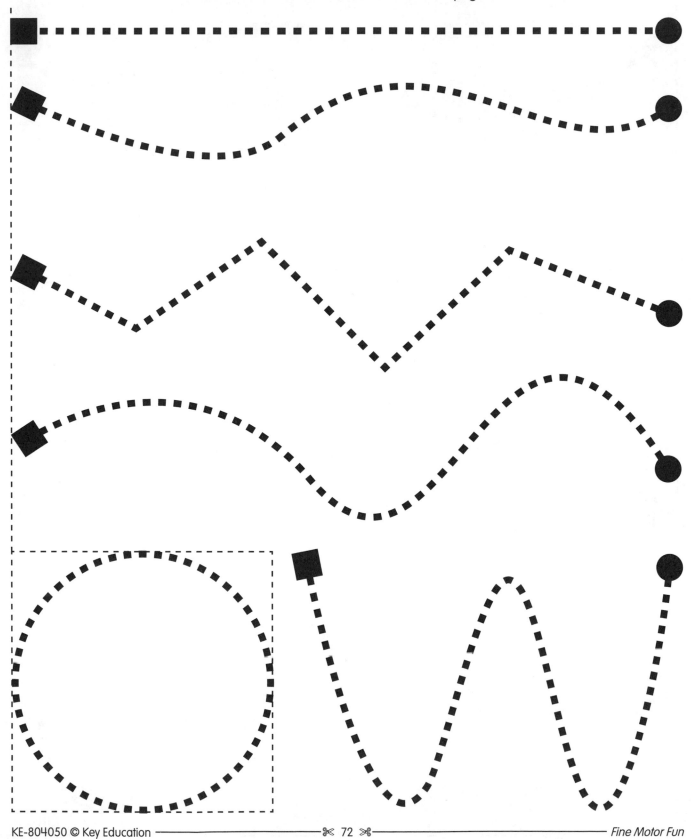

Coloring, Tracing, and Painting

Activities to Help Children Learn to Use Writing Tools

When children have acquired a certain amount of body stability and their hands and fingers have begun to work together, they will be ready to begin using a variety of coloring, drawing, and painting tools. Practicing with a variety of tools is an excellent prerequisite to using a pencil. The following ideas will increase eye-hand coordination, will help develop visual skills, and will prepare children for learning how to hold and use a pencil properly and learning how to print.

You should notice that when children first begin to use crayons to color, that often they will color using whole arm movements. Eventually, as they mature and their skills increase, the arm movements will change to wrist and then to finger movements.

- Fine motor skills are best developed when children work on vertical or near vertical surfaces, such as chalkboards, easels, lite-brights, magnets on refrigerators, wipe-off boards, or flannel boards.

- Attach a large sheet of paper to a wall, chalkboard, or bulletin board. The teacher should draw a line or a simple outline and then have the child trace over what the teacher has drawn using a large piece of chalk, crayon, or marker. After the child has traced the outline several times ask him to draw the same outline next to yours.

- Draw large dots on a black board, easel, or chart paper. Let the child have fun connecting the dots in any direction. There should be no right or wrong ways to connect the dots.

- Provide many tools for children to practice their fine motor skills: crayons, markers, colored glue, paint, watercolors, colored pencils, colored chalk, and bingo markers for dabbing color.

- Let the children use blackboards, easels, and chart paper to experiment with writing. Encourage children to draw shapes, lines, curved lines, and objects. Many young children will want to draw pictures of their families, pets, and favorite toys.

Ice Cube Paint

You will need: An ice cube tray, food coloring, craft sticks, and paper.

What you do: Fill an ice cube tray with water. Add food coloring and a craft stick to each ice cube tray section. Place in the freezer until the colored water is frozen. Provide the child with paper and the frozen paint. Let the child move the "popsicle-like" frozen paint around the paper.

This is a unique painting experience for young children. Just make sure that no one tries to taste the frozen paint!

Frozen Rainbow Paint

You will need: An ice cube tray, liquid tempera paint, craft sticks, and paper.

What you do: In an ice cube tray, add a shallow layer of tempera paint and a craft stick to each of the ice cube sections. Place in the freezer until the first layer is becoming frozen. Then add another layer of a different colored paint and so on, until there are four to five layers of paint in each ice cube section.

Provide the children with paper and the frozen paint and let the children paint. As this paint begins to melt, the colors will become more and more intense.

Paint with Safe Smelling Glue

A creative way to jazz up plain old white glue and make a new way to paint is to add Kool-Aid® packets of various flavors *(colors)* into approximately ¼ cup of glue. Mix thoroughly with paint brushes and amazing colors will come through. The glue will smell great and it will be glossy when it dries. A wonderful sensory activity.

Reproducible Fun Coloring Pages

Here are some ideas for some creative *(and educational)* ways to use pages 75–82. Each of these pages are designed for young children to add color to.

Idea 1: Using white glue, trace around the edge of the picture and let dry. This will provide a raised border which makes it easier for the child to color within the lines. The child can color in the picture with crayons, markers, paint, or any medium of their choosing.

Idea 2: Glue yarn around the border of the picture. This will also provide a raised border to help guide the child's coloring.

Idea 3: After creating a glue or yarn border, let the child fill in the rest of the picture with colored glue. Apply the glue by squeezing some into the center of the section to be colored and then moving the glue around with a Q-tip or a small paint brush.

Idea 4: Fill in color in any of the reproducible pages with a bingo marker. The children can simply "dab" color in each section.

Abstract Art

Directions are on page 74.

Three Balloons

Directions are on page 74.

Yellow Duck

Directions are on page 74.

Mighty Mouse

Directions are on page 74.

Dino-Dinosaur
Directions are on page 74.

Candy House

Directions are on page 74.

Colorful Clown

Directions are on page 74.

Beautiful Butterfly

Directions are on page 74.

Learning to Use a Pencil

Before the Pencil – First Tactile Experiences

Before young children learn to print, it is important to provide them with a wide variety of tactile experiences. Tactile experiences allow children to "feel" shapes, letters, and numbers as they draw with their fingers. Tactile and multisensory experiences are wonderful for all children, but can be especially helpful for children who find visual-motor and fine motor tasks difficult.

Cookie Sheet Tracing - Dry Materials

Fill a cookie sheet with any of the following materials: rice, clean sand, salt, glitter, coffee, sugar, seeds, small beads, or oatmeal. Let the children draw and trace with their fingers. Draw specific shapes and then ask the child to try to copy the shape that you have drawn.

Easy-to-Make Finger Paint

You will need: liquid starch, powdered tempera paint, a large mixing bowl, a spoon or other utensil for stirring, and finger paint paper.

What you do: Add the powdered tempera paint to the liquid starch until you have achieved the desired color. That's it! You are ready to paint!

Helpful Hint: For an easier cleanup, add a small amount of liquid dish washing detergent to the finger paint. Although the cleanup is easier, make sure the children still wear a paint smock or one of dad's old shirts!

Remember: Always make sure that you are finger painting on the shiny side of the paper.

Super Smelly Finger Paint

You will need: wallpaper paste or wheat paste, water, food coloring, oil of wintergreen, a large mixing bowl, a spoon or other utensil for stirring, and finger paint paper.

What you do: Mix the wallpaper paste or wheat paste with water until you have a thin paste. Add the food coloring and a few drops of oil of wintergreen. For more fun, try adding other scents such as vanilla, peppermint, lemon, or almond.

Gritty Finger Paint

You will need: I cup flour, I cup water, food coloring, I to I ½ cups of salt or sand, large mixing bowl, a spoon or another utensil for stirring, and finger paint paper.

What you do: Combine the flour with the salt or sand. Add the water and stir until thoroughly mixed. Add the food coloring one drop at a time until you achieve the desired color.

Wonderful Whipped Cream Creations

You will need: Coolwhip™ whipped cream, food coloring, large mixing bowl, a spoon or another utensil for stirring, and thick paper or a paper plate.

What you do: Combine only a drop or two of food coloring with the whipped cream. Too much food coloring can make the whipped cream runny—and it is not good for children to consume too much food coloring. Just a taste, please!

Yummy Yogurt Finger Paint

You will need: ½ carton plain yogurt, ½ package flavored gelatin, a mixing bowl, a spoon or other utensil for stirring, and finger paint paper.

What you do: Mix all of the ingredients together and then use as finger paint on a paper plate or on wax paper. A "healthy-to-taste" art experience! (Yummy Yogurt Finger Paint and Giggle Jiggle Gelatin Finger Paint are "edible" recipes. This does not mean that the children can consume an entire art experience. Edible recipes are meant just to be tasted! Also, remind the children to wash their hands before they create any edible art experience.)

Giggly Jiggly Gelatin Finger Paint

You will need: flavored gelatin, 9" x 13" pan, a mixing bowl, a spoon or other utensil for stirring, and finger paint paper.

What you do: Mix the gelatin according to the package directions. Place the gelatin in the refrigerator until it has a "gooey" consistency! Now use the gelatin to finger paint. Icky—sticky hilarious fun!

Super Sticky Finger Paint

You will need: corn syrup, food coloring, various containers for storing paint, mixing bowls, a spoon or other utensil for stirring, and finger paint paper.

What you do: Mix the corn syrup with only a drop or two of food coloring. Mix well and then store in air-tight containers or zip-sealed plastic bags. You can create a variety of colors and store for future use. This finger paint is very sticky when wet, but when it dries it will no longer feel sticky and it will look incredibly shiny.

WARNING! Anytime a flavored gelatin is used it will stain fingertips (which will eventually come clean), and it can stain clothes and laminated counters. Be careful — but have fun!

Silky Smooth Finger Paint

You will need: ¼ cup salt, 2 tablespoons cornstarch, 1 cup water, a pan, a spoon or other utensil for stirring, and finger paint paper.

What you do: Mix the water, salt, and cornstarch in a pan and bring it to a boil. Keep stirring until the mixture is the consistency of yogurt. If you want to make a variety of colors, divide the mixture and place it in different containers and add the food coloring. When cool, this mixture will feel smooth and silky.

Helpful Hint: This paint will last several weeks if it is put in tightly sealed containers or plastic bags and stored in a refrigerator.

Learning How to Hold a Pencil Properly

Some children just naturally know how to hold a pencil properly. Unfortunately, some children struggle to learn this skill and must be taught proper pencil grasp. Below are some tips that will help you teach pencil skills.

- **Good Posture.** Children should maintain good posture when they are learning how to print. Their feet should be on the floor and the desk surface should be at a height for the arm and elbow to rest comfortably. Ankles, hips, and knees should all be at 90 degree angles. If the chair is too high, place a foot stool under the child's feet.

- **Slanted Surface.** Learning how to print is easier when children are permitted to work on a slanted surface. Place a 4-inch three ring-binder on the desk in front of the child. The spine of the binder should be facing the top of the desk. Rotate the binder to a 45 degree angle. Tape a piece of writing paper on the binder. Writing on this slanted surface is fun and can be extremely beneficial.

- **Align Paper.** Even if you do not use a slanted surface, be sure that the paper is aligned parallel to the arm of the dominant hand and is at a 45 degree angle. The non-dominant hand should be used to hold the paper stable.

- **Proper Pencil Grasp.** The pencil should be held between the pads of the thumb and the index finger while resting on the middle finger. Another appropriate version of this grasp is for the pencil to be held between the pads of the thumb and the index and middle fingers while resting on the ring finger.

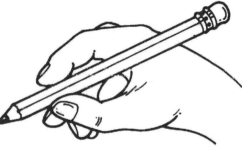

Extra Helpful Tips:

- **Pencil Grips.** Use pencil grips for children who have a difficult time remembering how to hold their pencil.

- **Short Pencils.** Break or sharpen pencils down to about a 2-inch length. This will encourage small hands to hold the pencil properly.

- **Chubby Writing Tools.** Use sidewalk chalk, chubby crayons, or a chubby pencil cut down to a short 2-inch length to help children gain more control.

First Drawing and Pencil Experiences

The following activities will help children gain more pencil control and increase early writing skills.

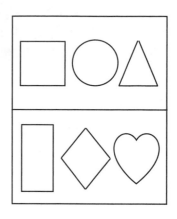

Make Your Own Stencils

Have fun playing with stencils. Reproducible stencil patterns can be found on pages 87–89. There are several ways to use stencils. First have the child hold the stencil with the non-dominant hand, while the dominate hand traces around the inside edge of the stencil to complete the picture or shape. It is also fun to hold the stencil with the non-dominant hand while the dominate hand dabs paint or colors over the entire space inside the stencil.

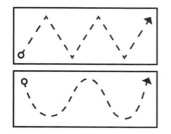

Make Your Own Tracing Cards

Reproducible tracing cards can be found on pages 90 and 91. Copy the pages onto heavy card stock, cut out along the dotted lines, and laminate for durability. Children can practice tracing over the lines with crayon and then erase what they have drawn with a tissue. These cards can be used over and over again.

Rainbow Writing

Most children really enjoy this activity. Provide each child with a page of shapes, letters, numbers, designs or a card with their name on it. Have the child trace over the images several times, each time using a different color crayon.

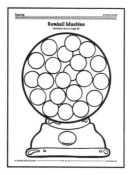

Pencil Paintings

Reproducible patterns have been provided on pages 92–94 for this activity. Fill several small containers, or a muffin tin, with a variety of colors of tempera paint. The children will dip the eraser end a pencil into the paint and then "dab" the color on the picture. When completed, the pictures will look like "pointillism. This will help children learn control and increase eye-hand coordination.

Crayon Rubbings

There are many different kinds of templates that can be commercially purchased. Place the template under a piece of paper and have the child "rub" crayon over the template. A picture of the template image will magically appear. Teachers can also prepare their own templates by cutting shapes out of plastic lids (margarine lids, coffee lids, plastic bottles.) Leaves, coins, and embossed greeting cards also work well as templates.

Stencil Patterns: Shapes

Directions are on page 86.

Stencil Patterns: Animals

Directions are on page 86.

(cut out)

(cut out)

(cut out)

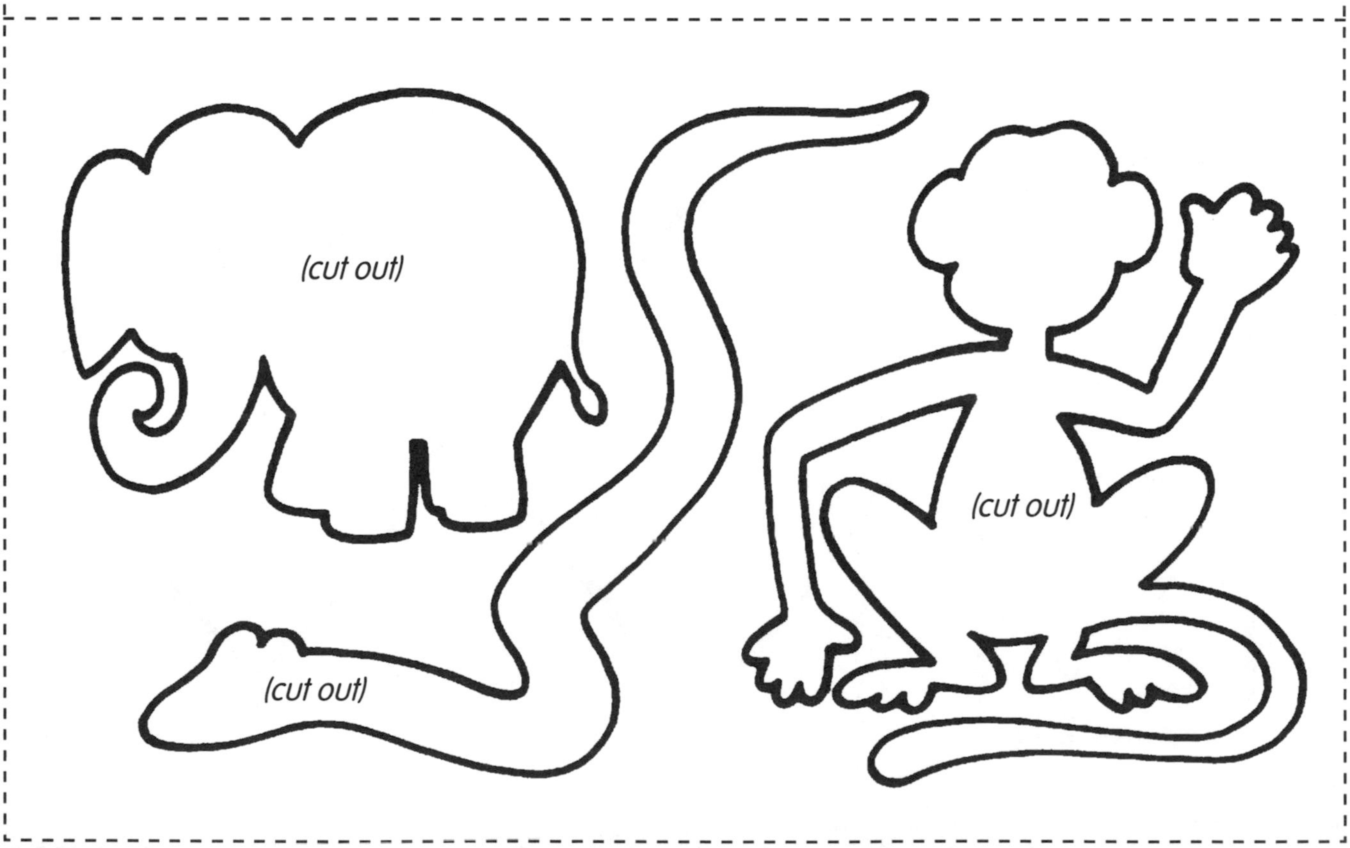

(cut out)

(cut out)

(cut out)

Stencil Patterns: Objects

Directions are on page 86.

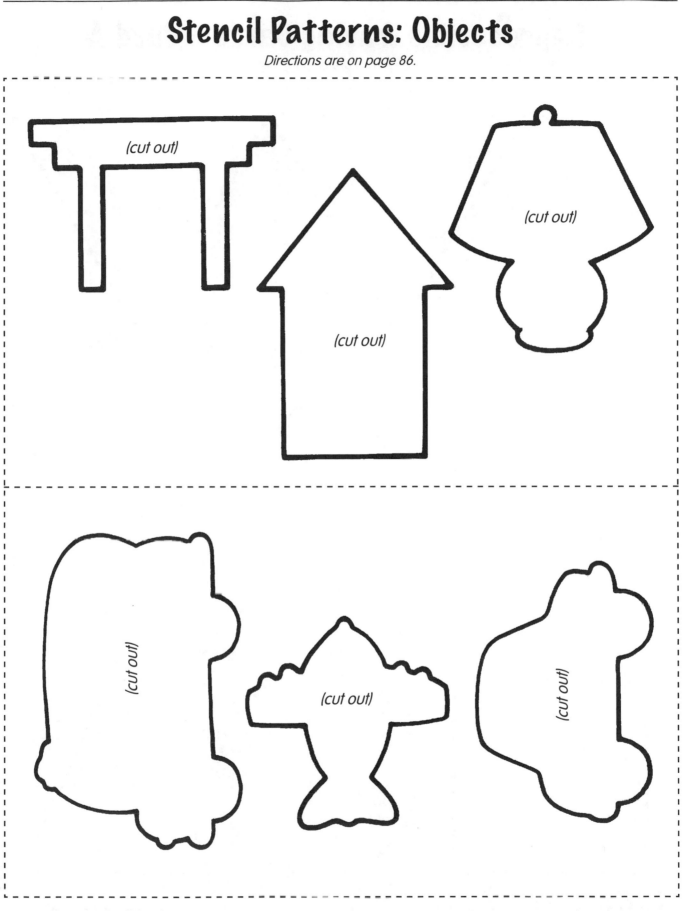

Reproducible Tracing Cards – Card A

Directions are on page 86.

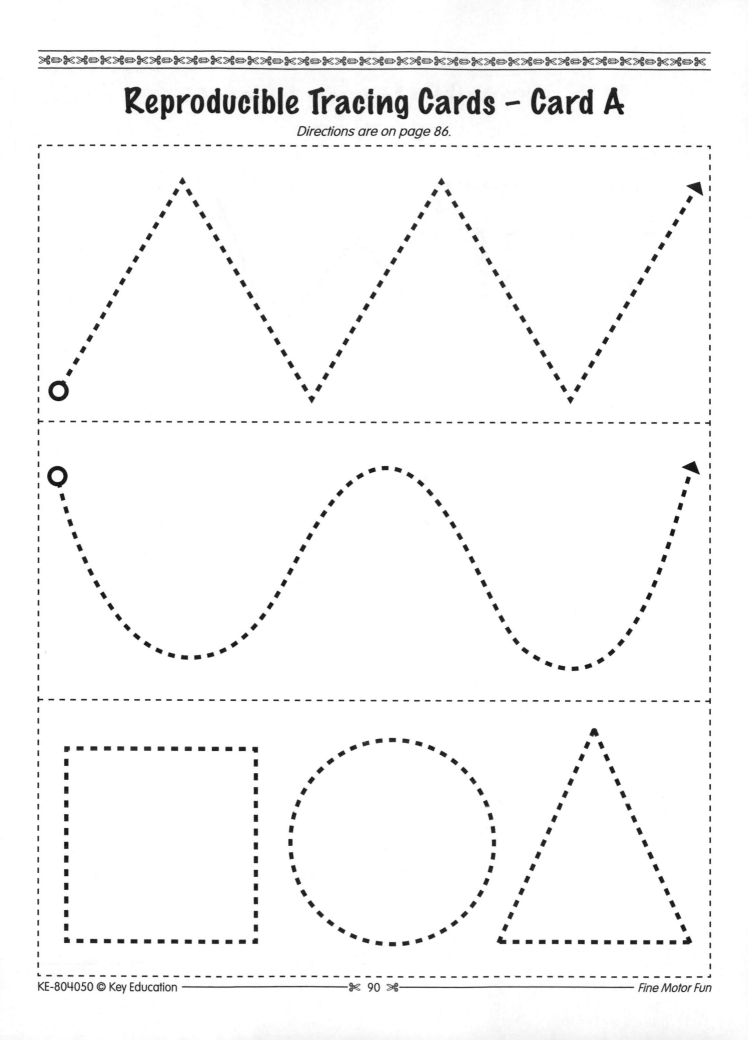

Reproducible Tracing Cards – Card B

Directions are on page 86.

Gumball Machine

Directions are on page 86.

Under the Sea

Directions are on page 86.

Up in the Sky

Directions are on page 86.

Learning to Trace and Draw with Pencils

Directions: Draw a straight line inside each pencil.

Crayons

Directions: Draw a straight line inside each crayon.

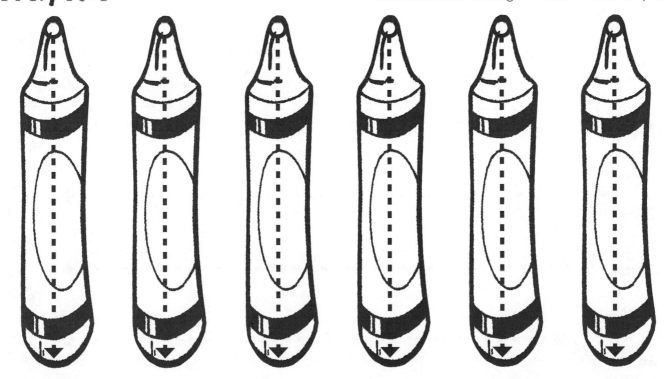

Flowers

Directions: Draw a straight line along each stem.

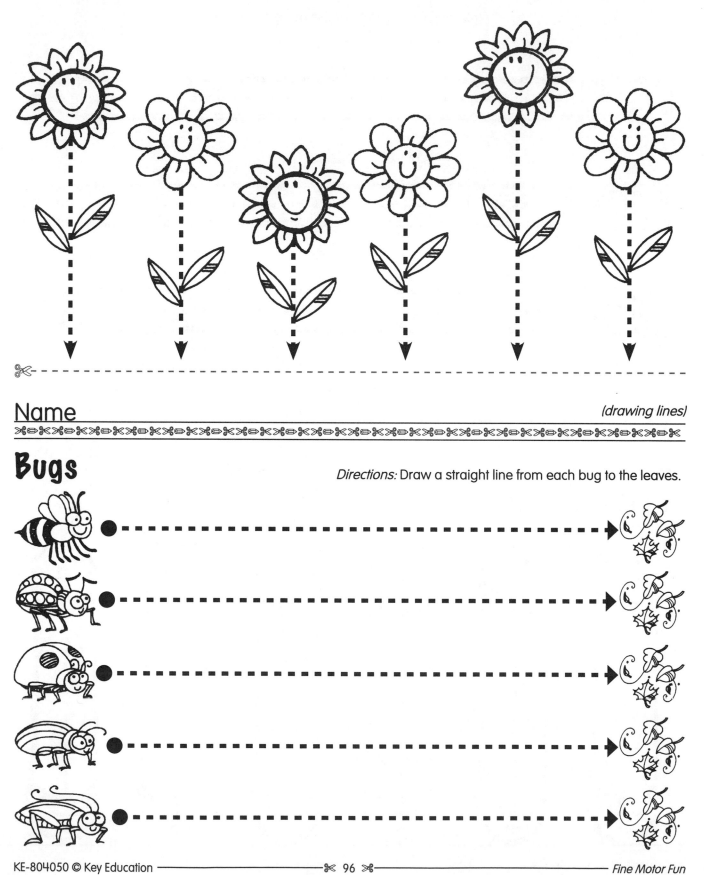

Bugs

Directions: Draw a straight line from each bug to the leaves.

Funny Frogs

Directions: Draw a line along each path.

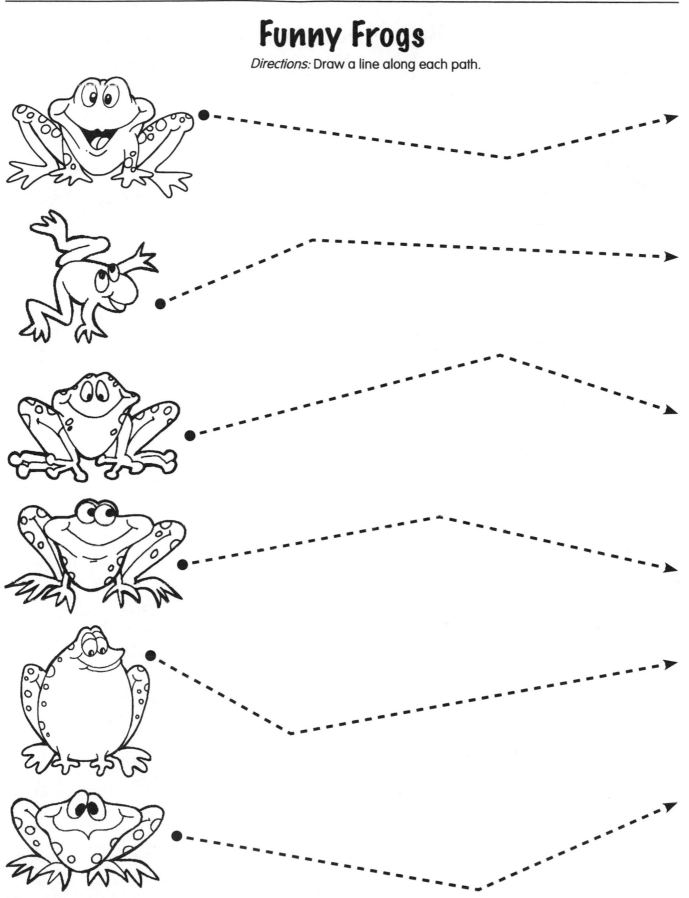

Skateboard Fun

Directions: Draw a line along each path.

Mice

Directions: Draw a line from each mouse to the cheese.

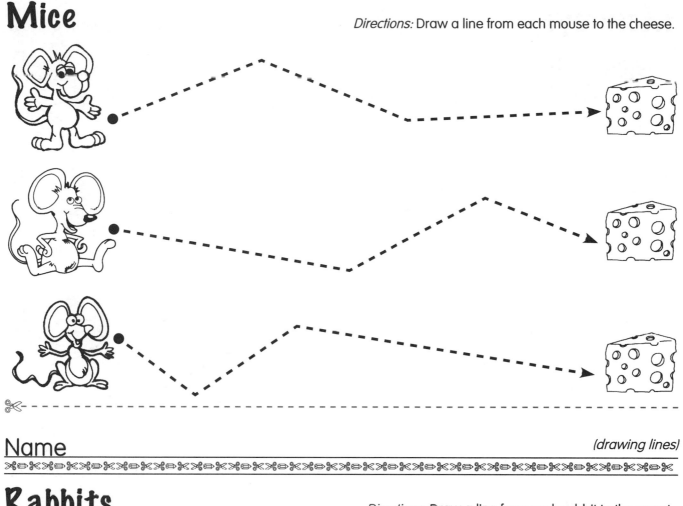

Rabbits

Directions: Draw a line from each rabbit to the carrot.

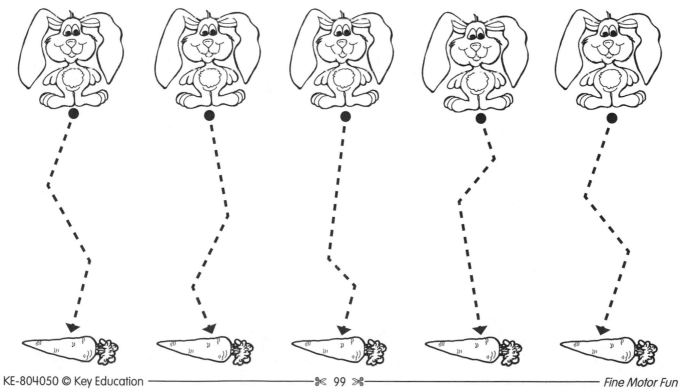

Monkeys

Directions: Draw a line from each monkey to the bananas.

Toucans

Directions: Draw a line from each toucan to the leaves.

Tickets

Directions: Draw lines to connect the dots to finish each ticket.

Photo Gallery

Directions: Draw lines to connect the dots to finish each frame.

Map 1

Directions: Draw lines to discover tthe treasure.

✂- -

Map 2

Directions: Draw lines to discover where you are.

Whale

Directions: Trace over the dotted lines.

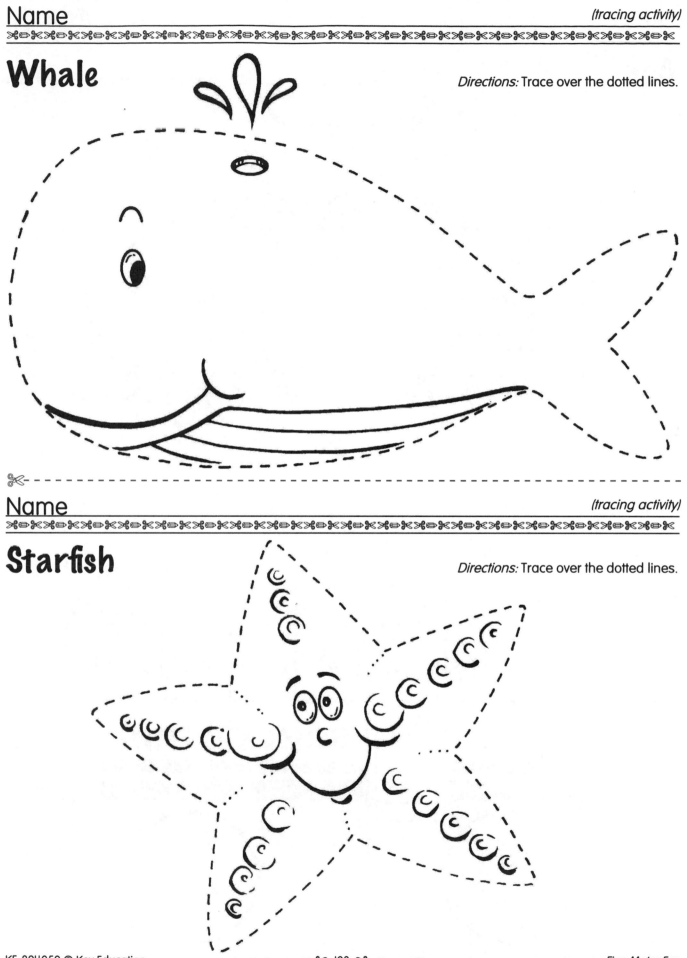

Starfish

Directions: Trace over the dotted lines.

Car

Directions: Trace over the dotted lines.

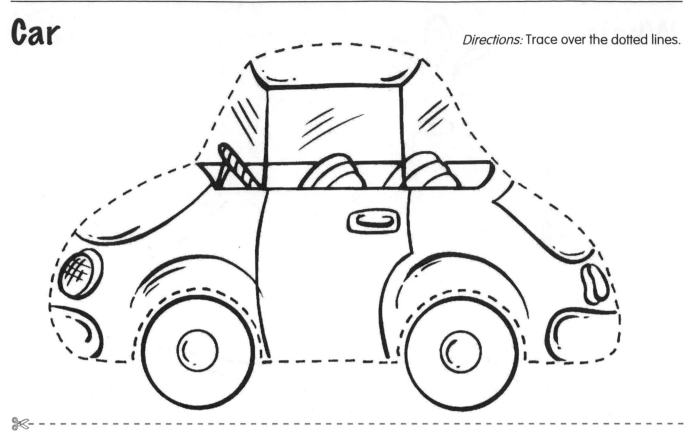

✂ -

Bus

Directions: Trace over the dotted lines.

SCHOOL BUS

(tracing activity)

Pig

Directions: Trace over the dotted lines.

(tracing activity)

Sheep

Directions: Trace over the dotted lines.

Bird

Directions: Trace over the dotted lines.

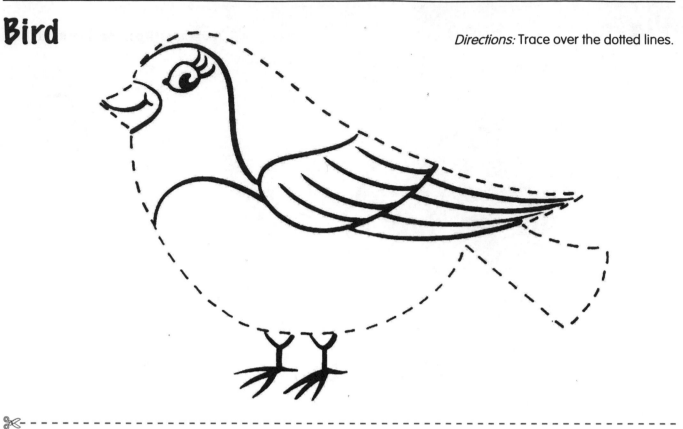

✂- -

Owl

Directions: Trace over the dotted lines.

Name _____ *(tracing activity)*

Dog

Directions: Trace over the dotted lines.

Name _____ *(tracing activity)*

Cat

Directions: Trace over the dotted lines.

Jack-In-The-Box

Directions: Draw lines to connect the dots in numerical order.

━━━ ✄ 108 ✄ ━━━

Fishbowl

Directions: Draw lines to connect the dots in numerical order.

Sailboat

Directions: Draw lines to connect the dots in numerical order.

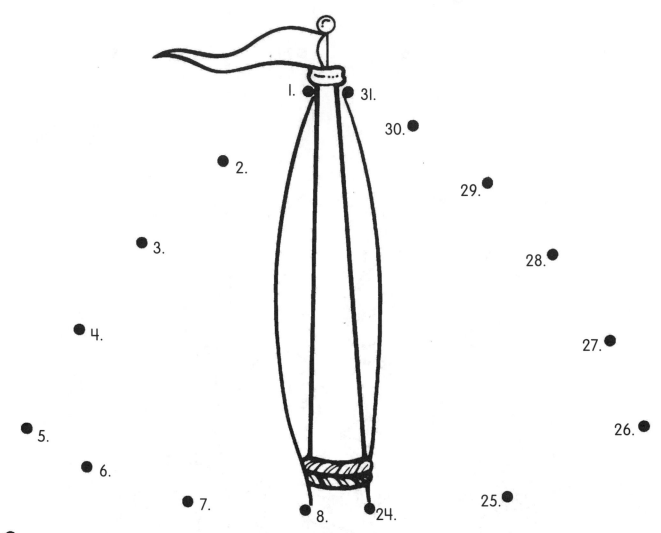

1. 31.
2. 30.
   29.
   28.
3. 27.
4. 26.
5. 25.
6. 8. 24.
7.
12. 20.
11. 21.
10. 9. 23. 22.
13. 19.
14. 18.
15. 16. 17.

Castle

Directions: Draw lines to connect the dots in numerical order.

Finish the Design – 4 Dots

Directions: Draw the same design by connecting the dots.

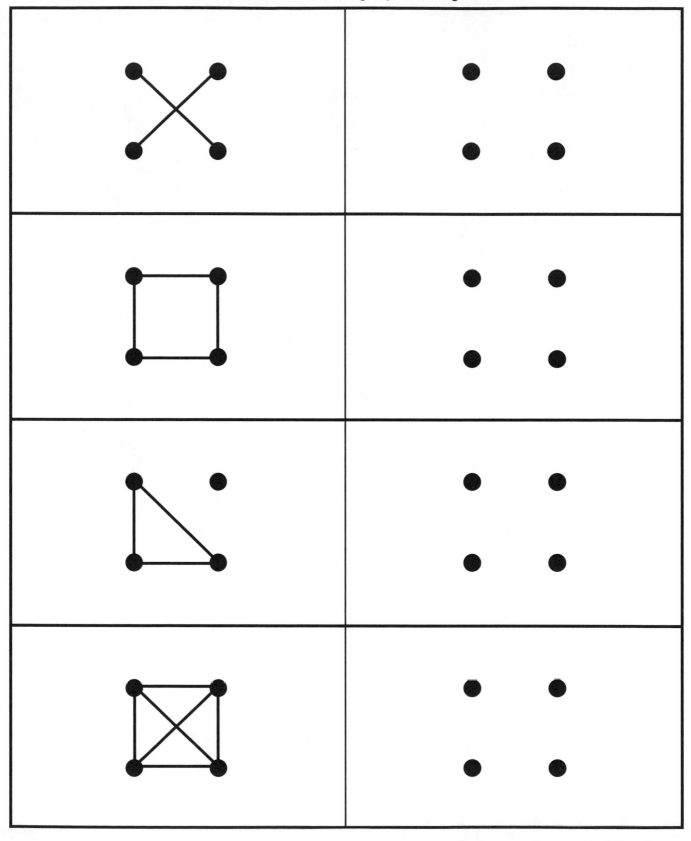

Finish the Design – 6 Dots

Directions: Draw the same design by connecting the dots.

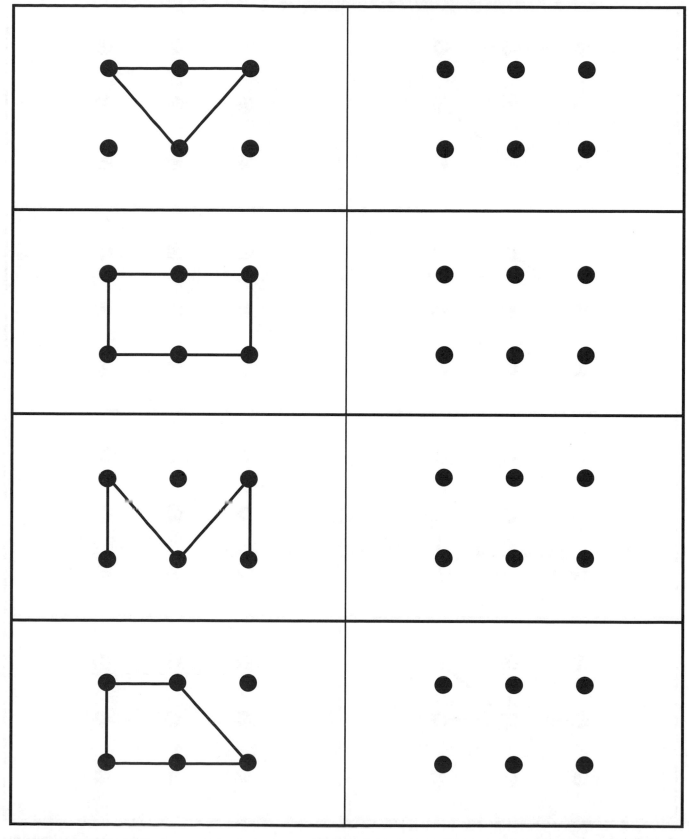

Finish the Design – 9 Dots

Directions: Draw the same design by connecting the dots.

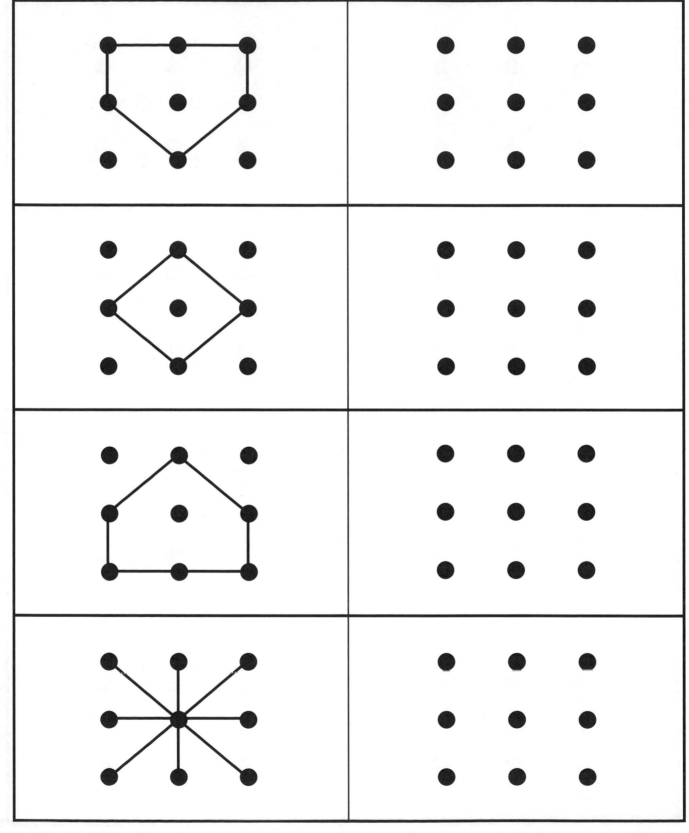

Finish the Design - 12 Dots

Directions: Draw the same design by connecting the dots.

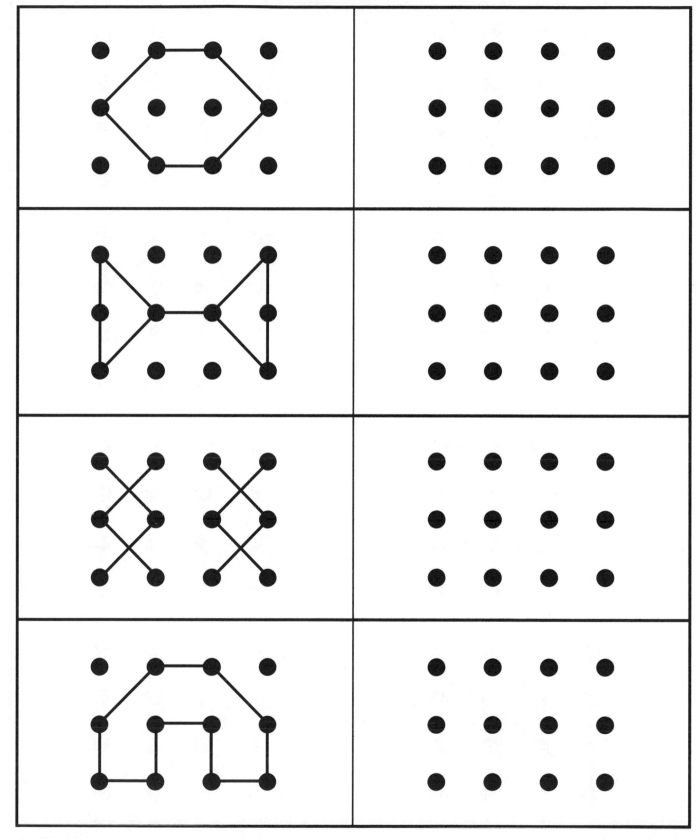

Finish the Design – 16 Dots

Directions: Draw the same design by connecting the dots.

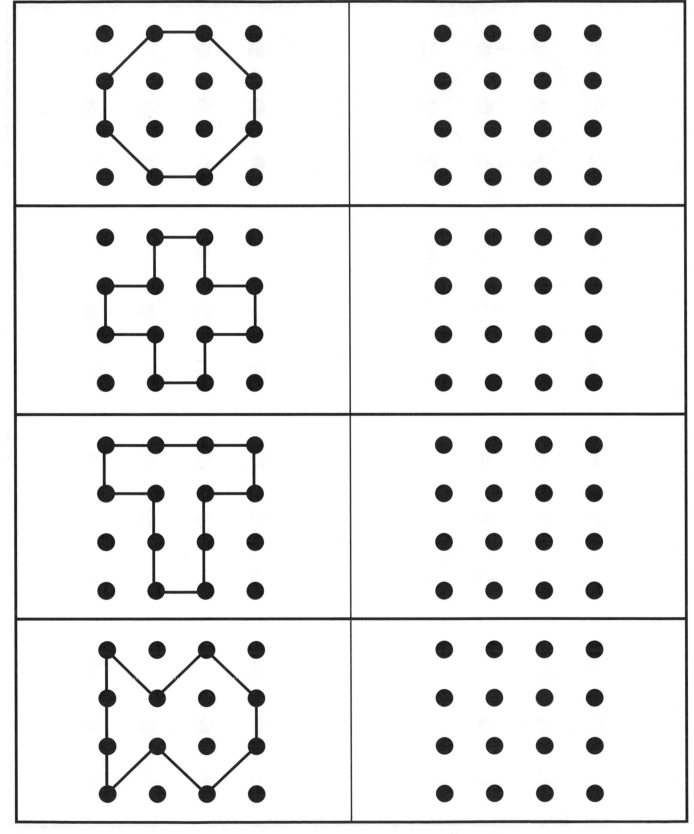

Help Red Riding Hood

Directions: Use your pencil. Help Red Riding Hood find her way home.

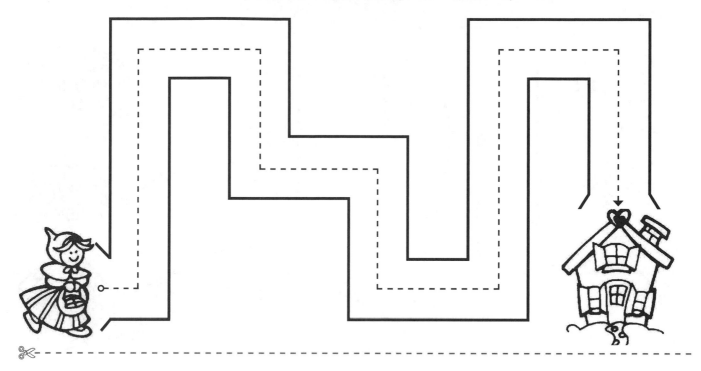

Help The Spider

Directions: Use your pencil. Help the Spider find Miss Muffet.

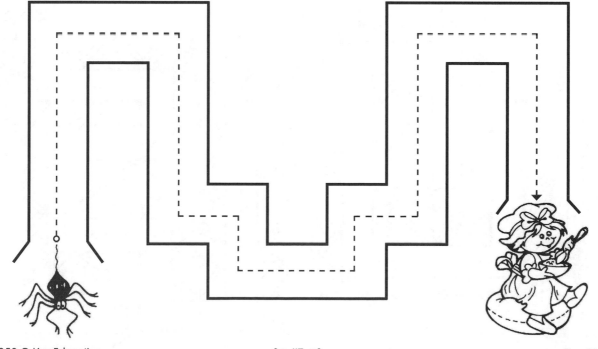

Help The Three Pigs

Directions: Use your pencil. Help the pigs find their homes.

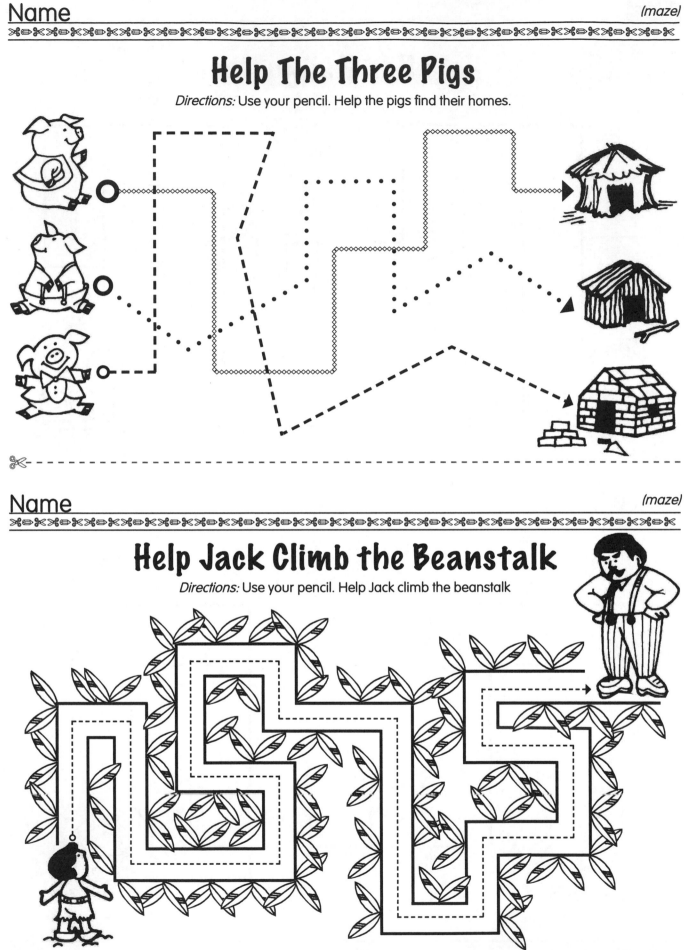

✂ -

Help Jack Climb the Beanstalk

Directions: Use your pencil. Help Jack climb the beanstalk

Help Hansel and Gretel

Directions: Use your pencil. Help Hansel and Gretel find their way home.

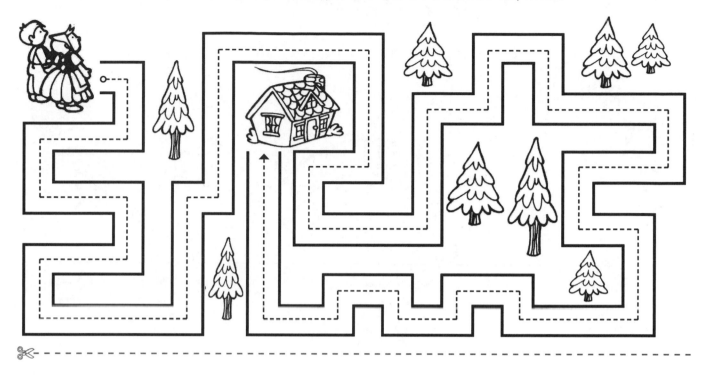

✂ -

Help the Cow Jump Over the Moon

Directions: Use your pencil. Help the cow jump over the moon.

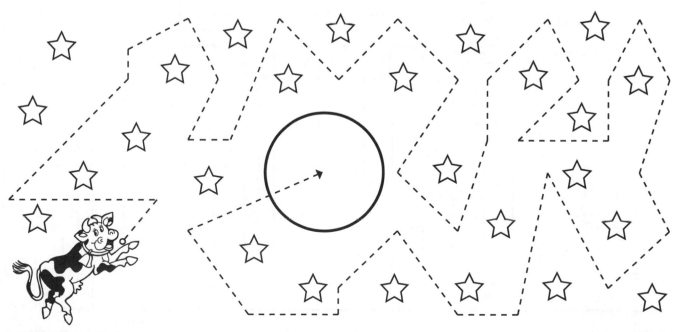

Help the Goats Trot Over the Bridge

Directions: Use a different color for each goat. Help the goats get over the bridge.

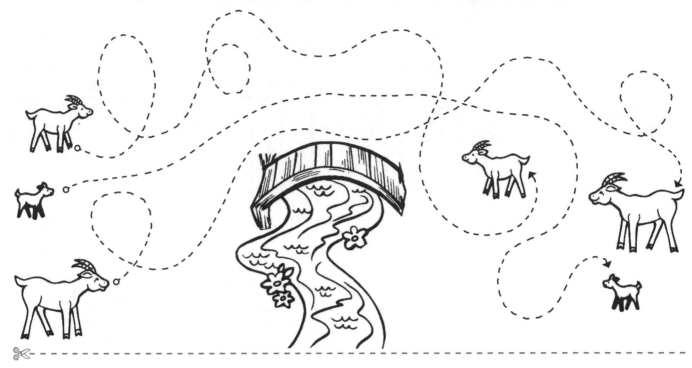

Help Wee Willie Winkie

Directions: Use your pencil. Help Wee Willie Winkie wake up the town.

Finish the Ladybug

Directions: Use your pencil. Finish drawing the ladybug.

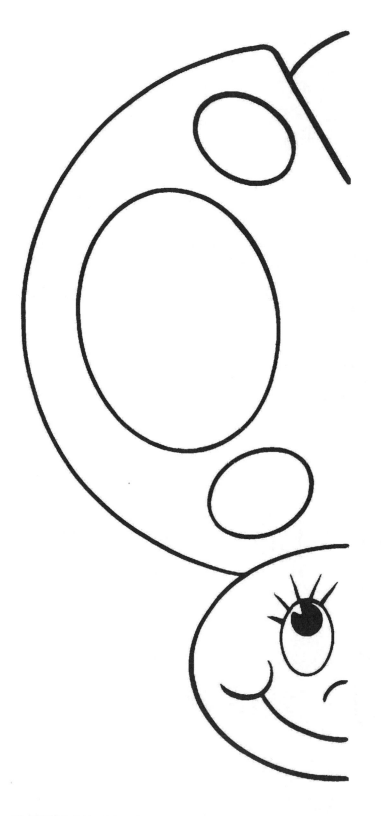

Finish the Bunny

Directions: Use your pencil. Finish drawing the bunny.

Finish the Puppy

Directions: Use your pencil. Finish drawing the puppy.

Finish the Elephant

Directions: Use your pencil. Finish drawing the elephant.

Learning to Print the Alphabet
Introduction to Basic Strokes

Learning how to print can either be a frustrating and challenging experience for a young child, or it can be a fun and successful experience. All of the activities in *Fine Motor Fun* have been designed to make learning how to print a successful experience.

So, what makes the difference? Often, teachers and parents present learning how to print letters in alphabetical sequence. Developmentally, this makes very little sense. Children need to learn how to control a pencil and how to make various handwriting strokes before they are able to print letters. *Fine Motor Fun* gives children the opportunity to learn how to control a pencil and then learn specific handwriting strokes, which then enables them to print a variety of alphabet letters.

First, children should be taught how to make "tall straight lines" and then "long straight lines." When children are able to print these lines they are then able to print "l, i, L, t, T, F, E, H, and I." Children immediately feel successful and are learning correct handwriting skills.

Children should be able to print the following strokes before alphabet letters are taught:

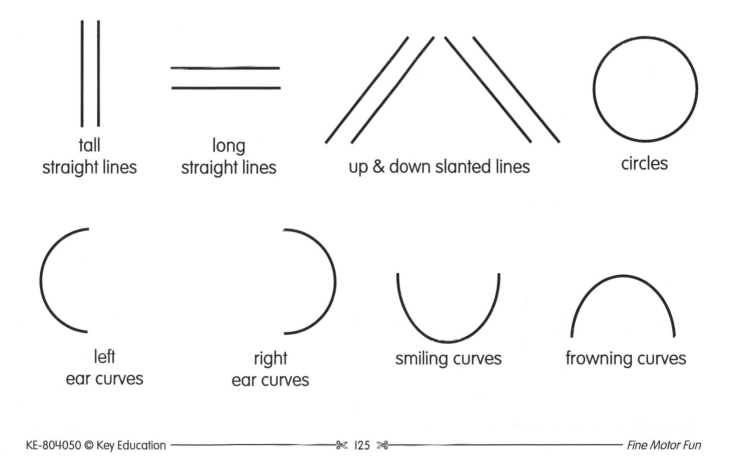

tall
straight lines

long
straight lines

up & down slanted lines

circles

left
ear curves

right
ear curves

smiling curves

frowning curves

Tall Straight Lines

Directions: Practice drawing tall straight lines. Make each line a different color.

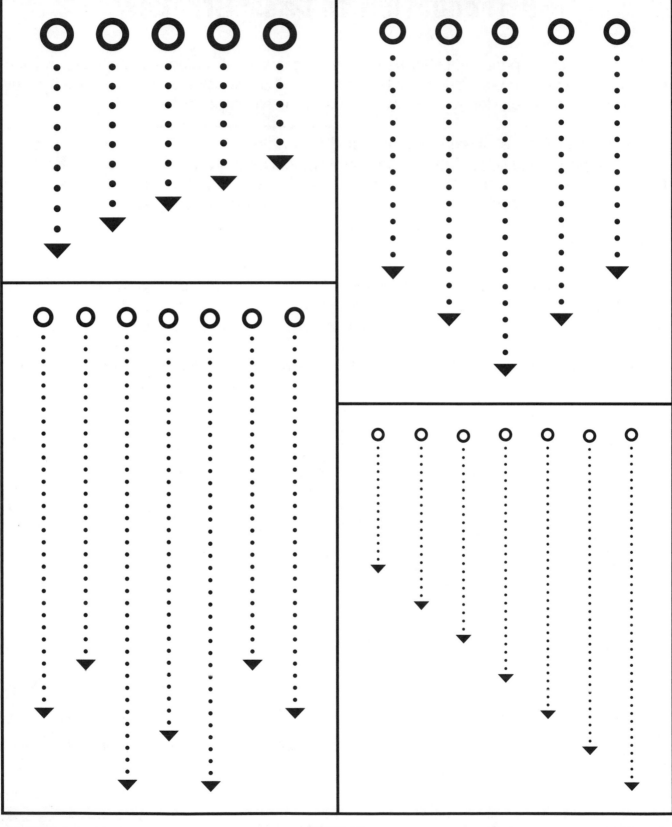

Name

Trace with glue. Add glitter.
Let dry. Trace with your fingertip.

Lowercase "l"

Trace.

Print your own.

✂ -

Name

Trace with glue. Add glitter.
Let dry. Trace with your fingertip.

Lowercase "i"

Trace.

Print your own.

Long Straight Lines

Directions: Practice drawing long straight lines. Make each line a different color.

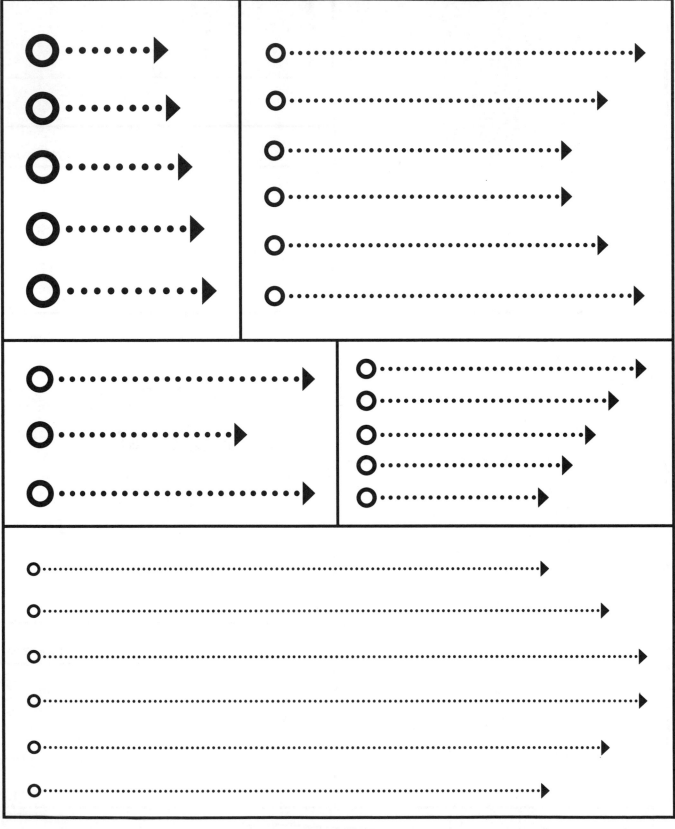

Trace with glue. Add glitter.
Let dry. Trace with your fingertip.

Uppercase "L"

Trace.

Print your own.

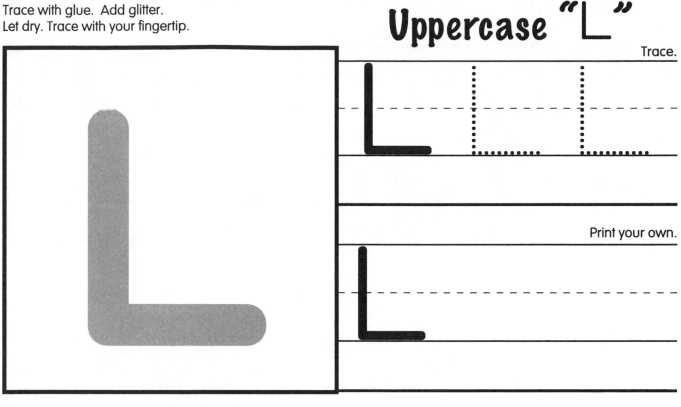

✂ -

Trace with glue. Add glitter.
Let dry. Trace with your fingertip.

Uppercase "T"

Trace.

Print your own.

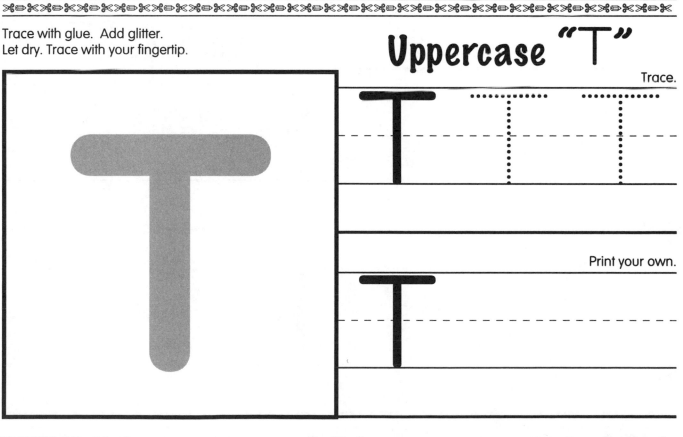

Name

Trace with glue. Add glitter.
Let dry. Trace with your fingertip.

Lowercase "t"

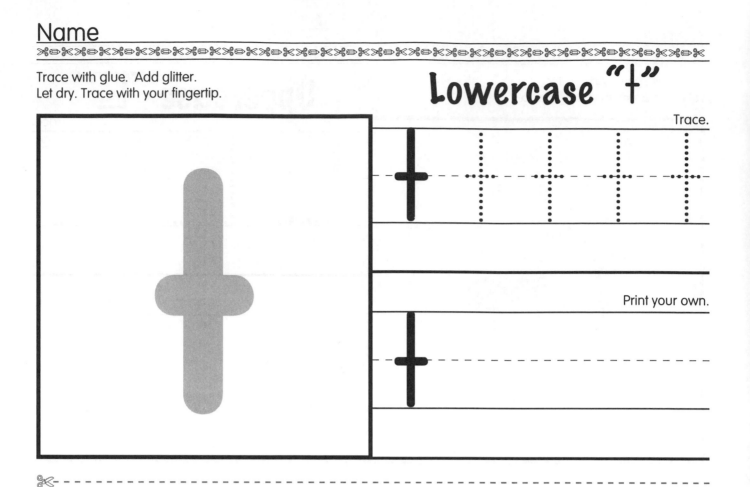

Trace.

Print your own.

Name

Trace with glue. Add glitter.
Let dry. Trace with your fingertip.

Uppercase "F"

Trace.

Print your own.

Name

Trace with glue. Add glitter.
Let dry. Trace with your fingertip.

Uppercase "E"

Trace.

E E E E E

Print your own.

E E

Name

Trace with glue. Add glitter.
Let dry. Trace with your fingertip.

Uppercase "H"

Trace.

H H H H H

Print your own.

H H

Up and Down Slanted Lines

Directions: Practice drawing up and down slanted lines.

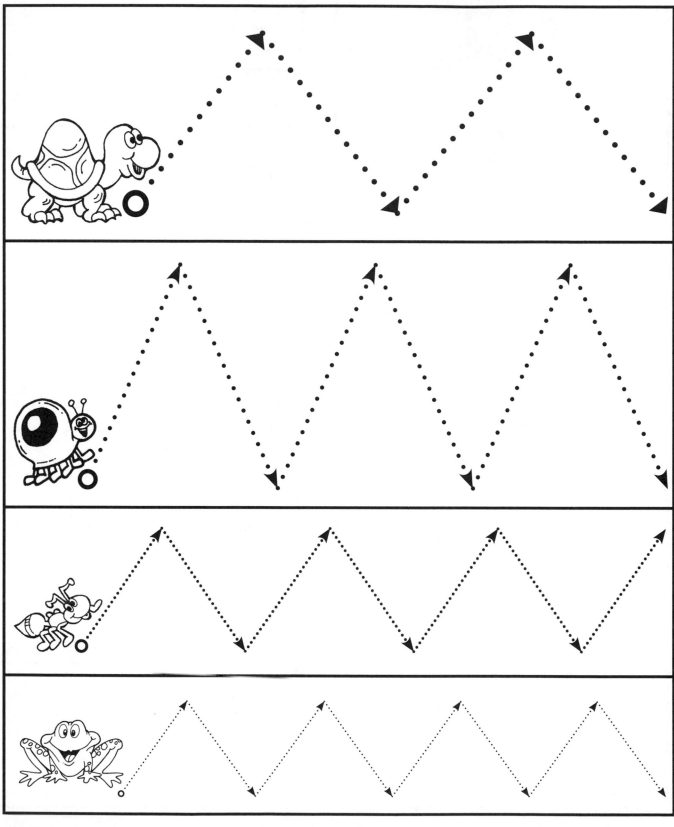

Up and Down Slanted Lines

Directions: Practice drawing up and down slanted lines.

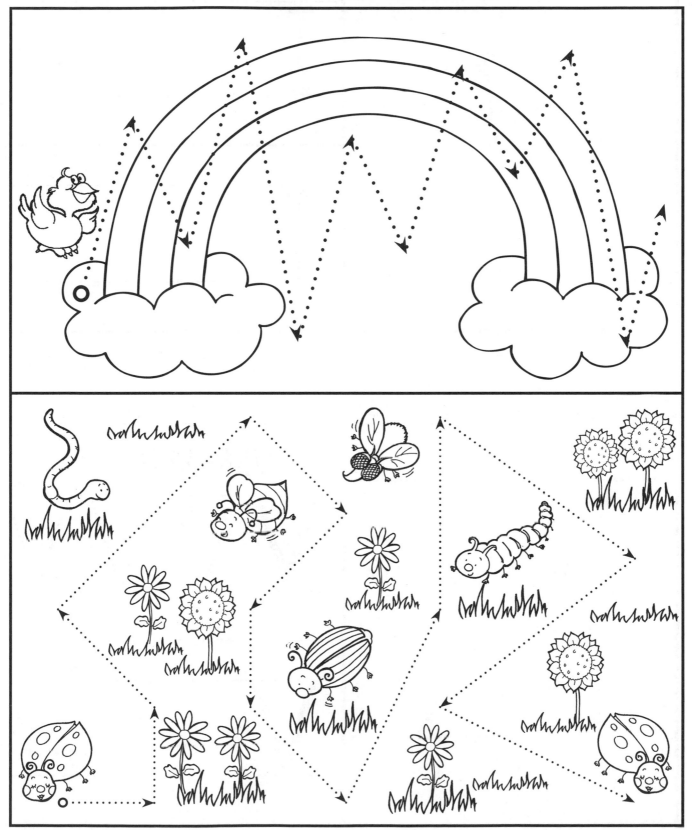

Name _____

Trace with glue. Add glitter.
Let dry. Trace with your fingertip.

Uppercase "I"

Trace.

Print your own.

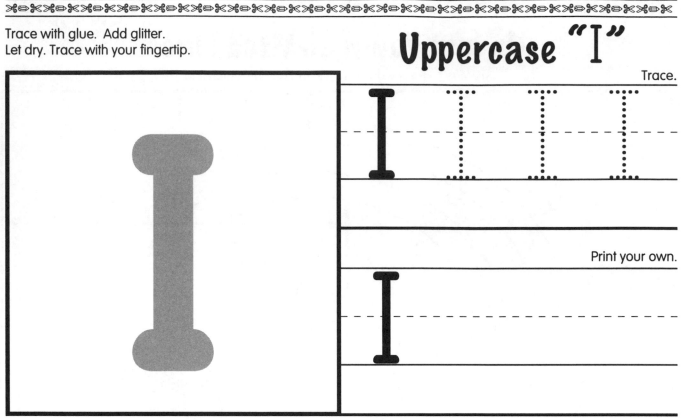

✂ -

Name _____

Trace with glue. Add glitter.
Let dry. Trace with your fingertip.

Uppercase "V"

Trace.

Print your own.

Name

Trace with glue. Add glitter.
Let dry. Trace with your fingertip.

Uppercase "N"

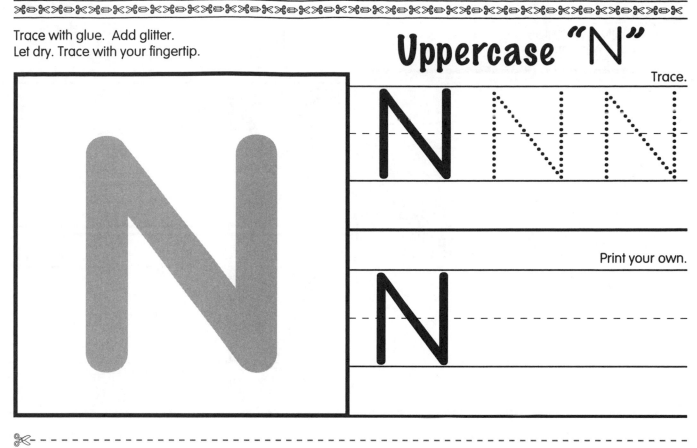

Trace.

Print your own.

Name

Trace with glue. Add glitter.
Let dry. Trace with your fingertip.

Uppercase "W"

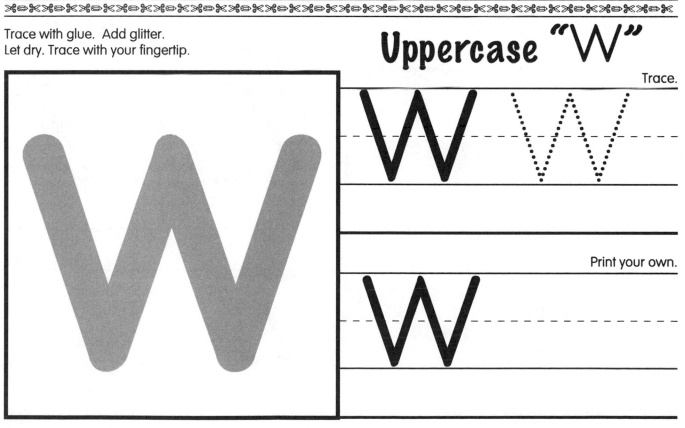

Trace.

Print your own.

<u>Name</u>

Trace with glue. Add glitter.
Let dry. Trace with your fingertip.

Uppercase "M"

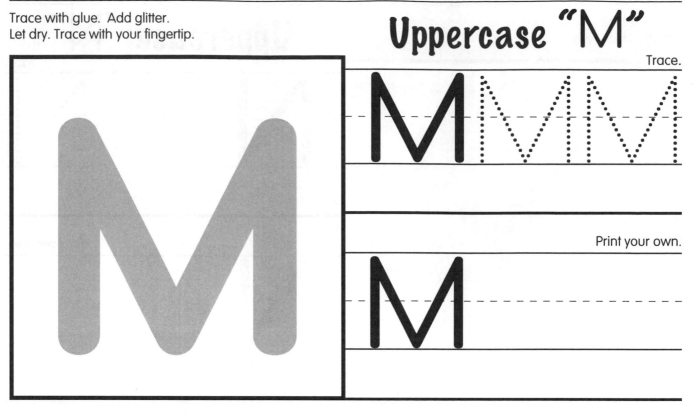

Trace.

Print your own.

✂ -

<u>Name</u>

Trace with glue. Add glitter.
Let dry. Trace with your fingertip.

Uppercase "Z"

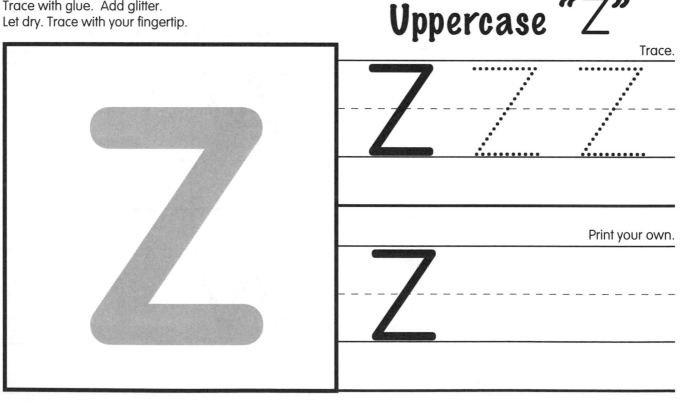

Trace.

Print your own.

Name _____

Trace with glue. Add glitter.
Let dry. Trace with your fingertip.

Uppercase "X"

Trace.

Print your own.

-✂--

Name _____

Trace with glue. Add glitter.
Let dry. Trace with your fingertip.

Uppercase "A"

Trace.

Print your own.

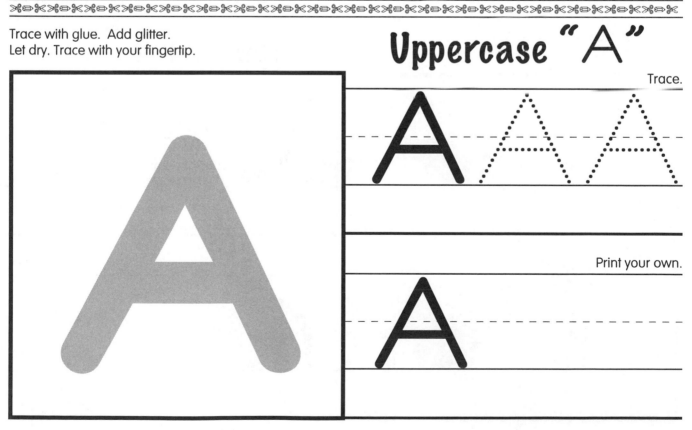

Name

Trace with glue. Add glitter.
Let dry. Trace with your fingertip.

Uppercase "Y"

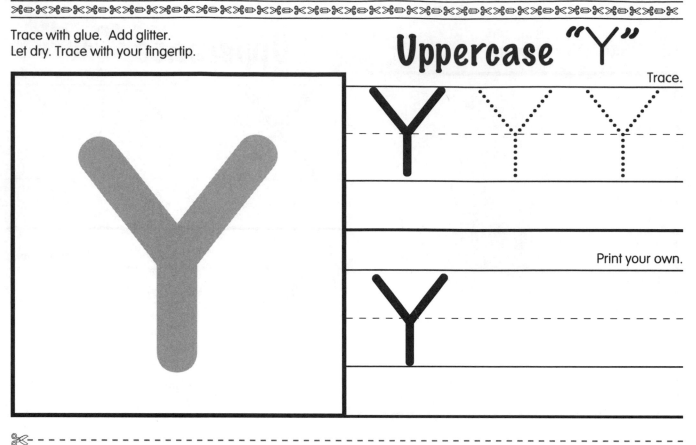

Trace.

Print your own.

- -

Name

Trace with glue. Add glitter.
Let dry. Trace with your fingertip.

Uppercase "K"

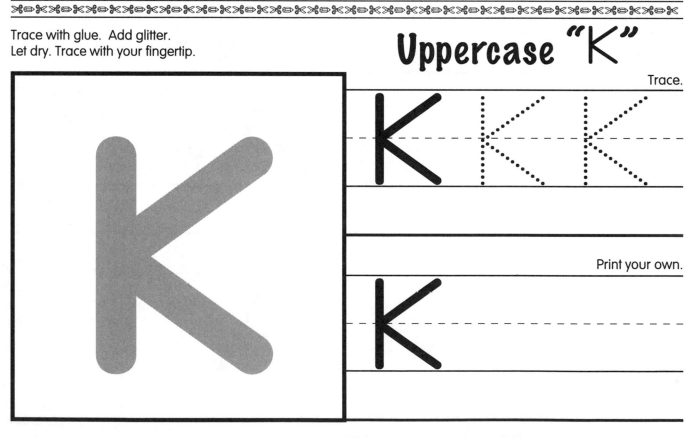

Trace.

Print your own.

Name

Trace with glue. Add glitter.
Let dry. Trace with your fingertip.

Lowercase "v"

Trace.

v v v v v

Print your own.

v

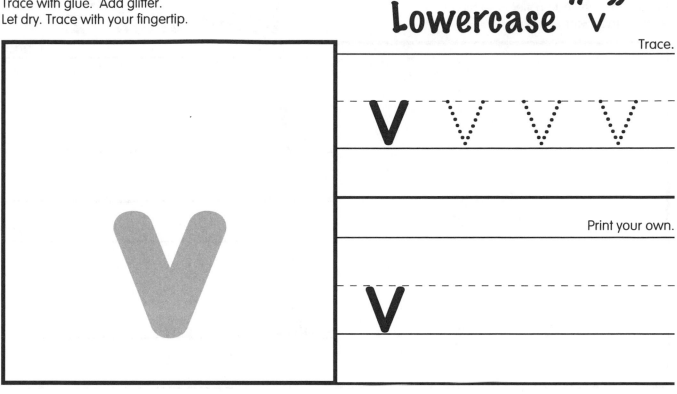

✂ -

Name

Trace with glue. Add glitter.
Let dry. Trace with your fingertip.

Lowercase "w"

Trace.

w w w w w

Print your own.

w

Name

Trace with glue. Add glitter.
Let dry. Trace with your fingertip.

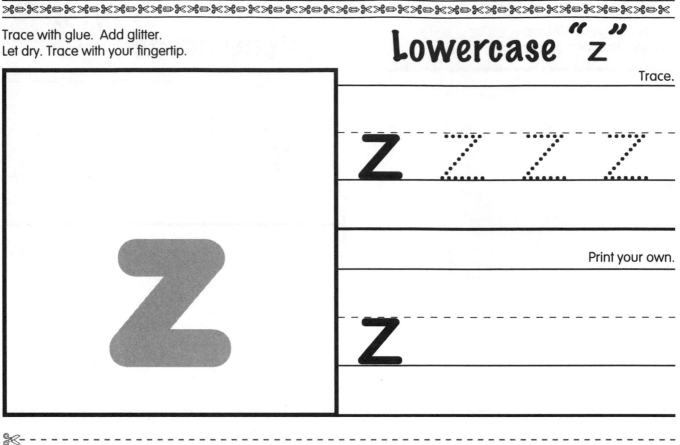

Lowercase "z"

Trace.

Print your own.

Name

Trace with glue. Add glitter.
Let dry. Trace with your fingertip.

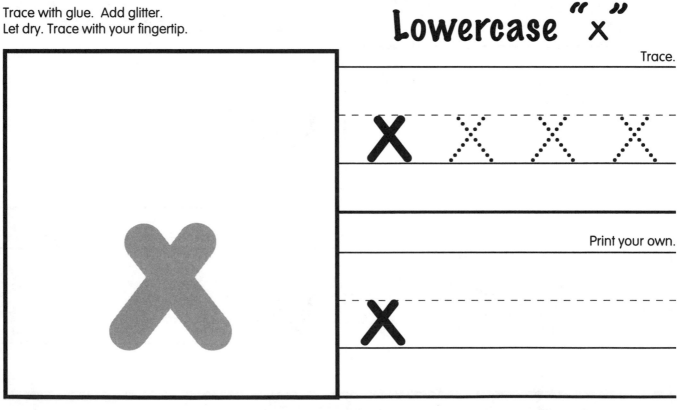

Lowercase "x"

Trace.

Print your own.

Name

Trace with glue. Add glitter.
Let dry. Trace with your fingertip.

Lowercase "y"

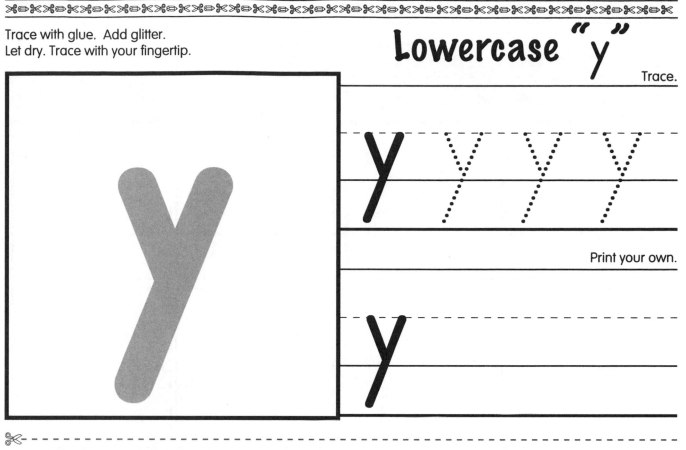

Trace.

Print your own.

✂ -

Name

Trace with glue. Add glitter.
Let dry. Trace with your fingertip.

Lowercase "k"

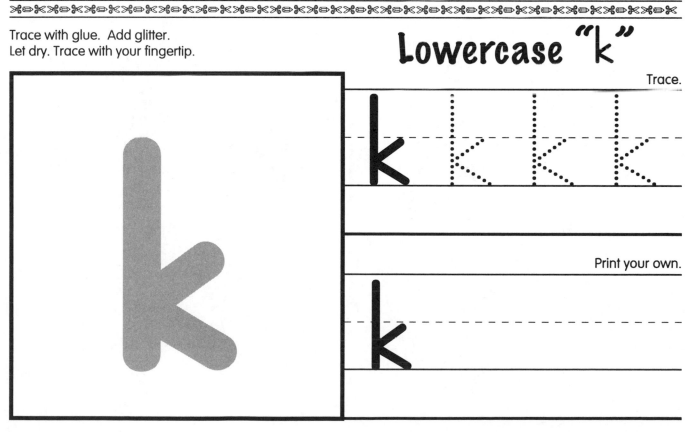

Trace.

Print your own.

Draw Circles

Directions: Draw a circle in each square.

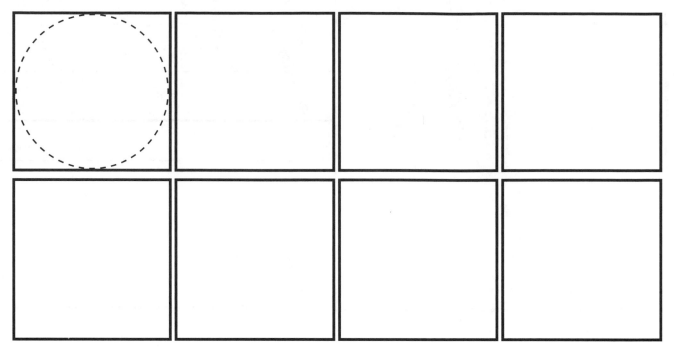

Directions: Draw a circle around each animal.

Name _____

Trace with glue. Add glitter.
Let dry. Trace with your fingertip.

Uppercase "O"

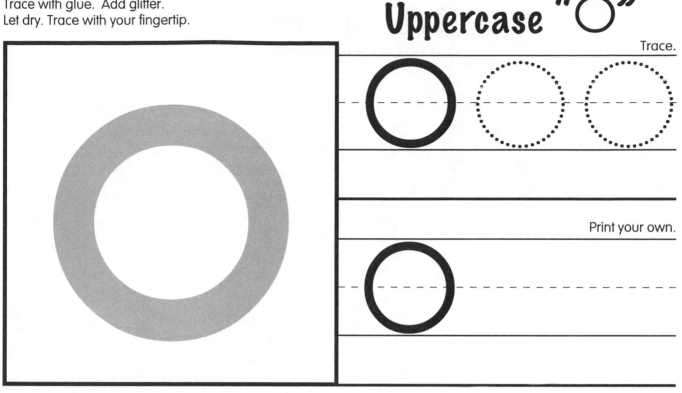

Trace.

Print your own.

✂ -

Name _____

Trace with glue. Add glitter.
Let dry. Trace with your fingertip.

Uppercase "Q"

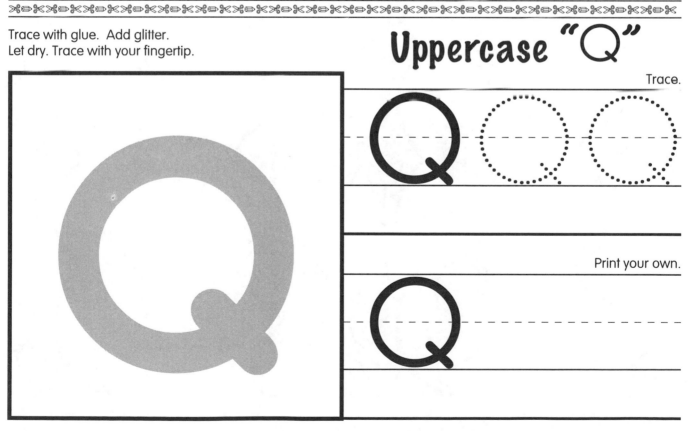

Trace.

Print your own.

Left Ear Curves

Directions: Practice drawing left ear curves

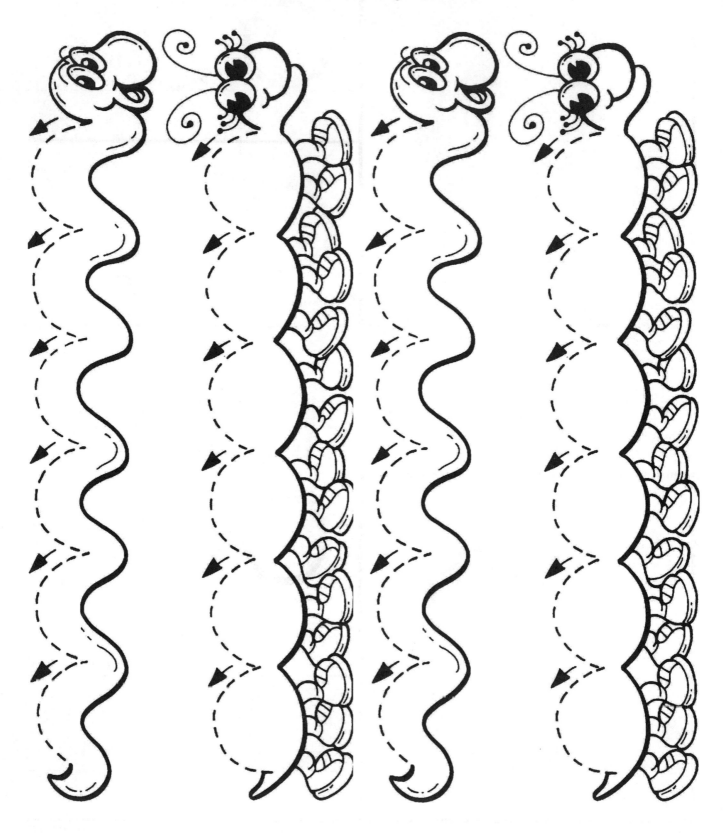

Name

Trace with glue. Add glitter.
Let dry. Trace with your fingertip.

Lowercase "o"

Trace.

Print your own.

Name

Trace with glue. Add glitter.
Let dry. Trace with your fingertip.

Uppercase "C"

Trace.

Print your own.

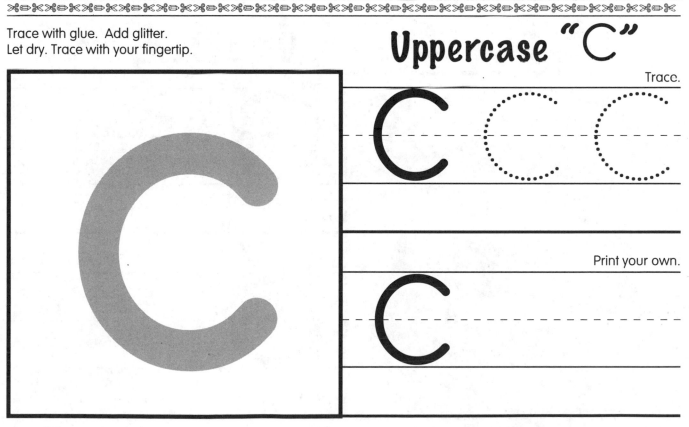

Trace with glue. Add glitter.
Let dry. Trace with your fingertip.

Lowercase "c"

Trace.

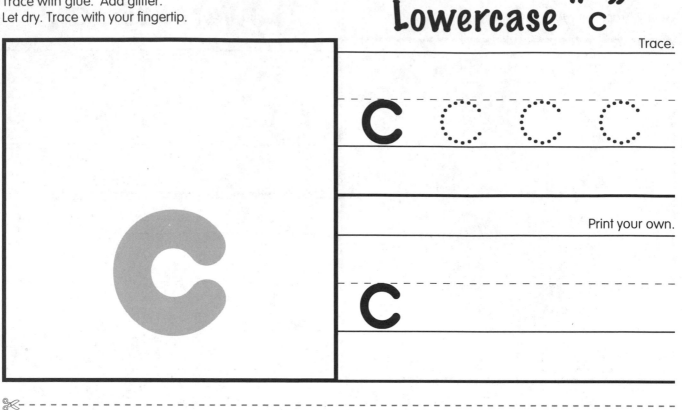

Print your own.

Trace with glue. Add glitter.
Let dry. Trace with your fingertip.

Uppercase "G"

Trace.

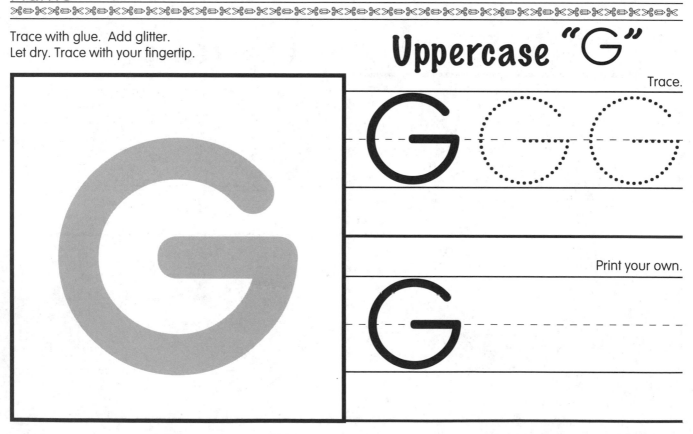

Print your own.

Name

Trace with glue. Add glitter.
Let dry. Trace with your fingertip.

Lowercase "a"

Trace.

a a a a

Print your own.

a

✂ -

Name

Trace with glue. Add glitter.
Let dry. Trace with your fingertip.

Lowercase "d"

Trace.

d d d d

Print your own.

d

Name

Trace with glue. Add glitter.
Let dry. Trace with your fingertip.

Lowercase "e"

Trace.

e · · · · · ·

Print your own.

e

✂ -

Name

Trace with glue. Add glitter.
Let dry. Trace with your fingertip.

Lowercase "g"

Trace.

g g g g

Print your own.

g

Right Ear Curves

Directions: Practice drawing right ear curves. Make each one a different color.

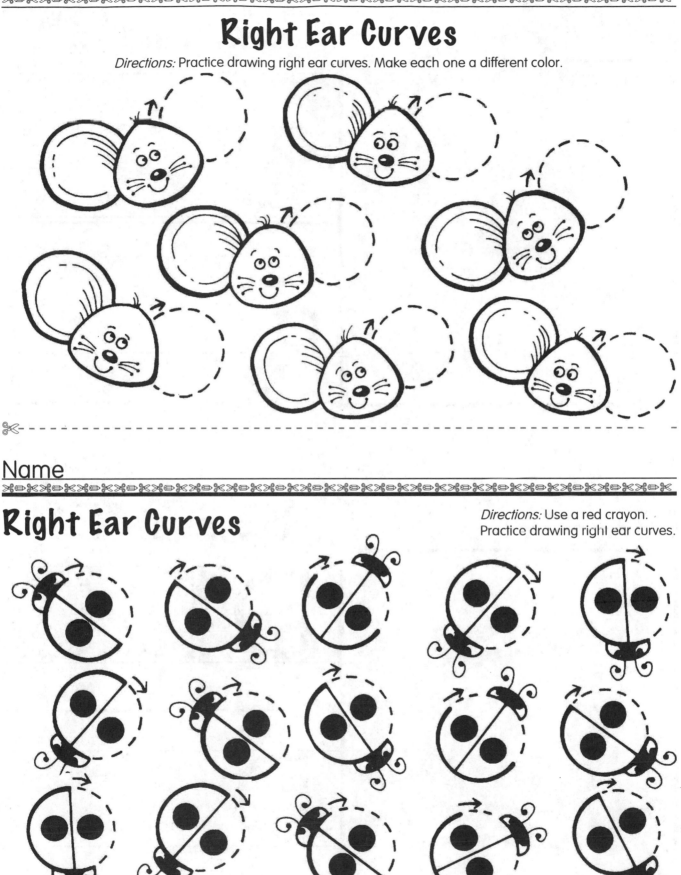

Right Ear Curves

Directions: Use a red crayon.
Practice drawing right ear curves.

Name

Trace with glue. Add glitter.
Let dry. Trace with your fingertip.

Lowercase "q"

Trace.

q   q q q q

Print your own.

q

Name

Trace with glue. Add glitter.
Let dry. Trace with your fingertip.

Uppercase "D"

Trace.

D   D D D

Print your own.

D

Name

Trace with glue. Add glitter.
Let dry. Trace with your fingertip.

Uppercase "P"

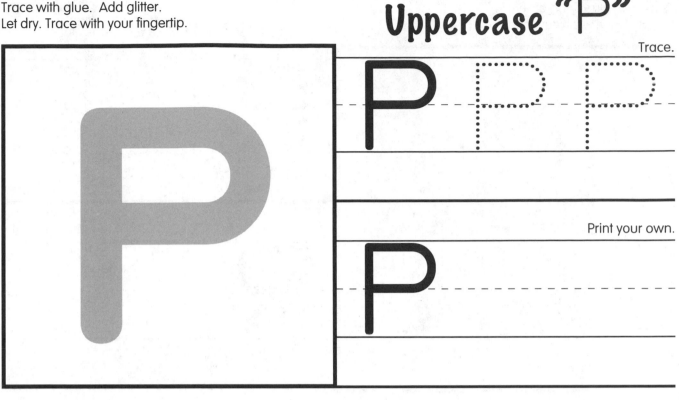

Trace.

Print your own.

Name

Trace with glue. Add glitter.
Let dry. Trace with your fingertip.

Uppercase "B"

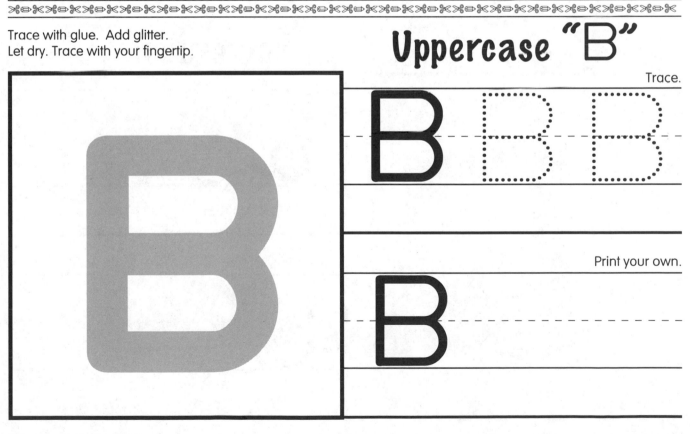

Trace.

Print your own.

Name

Trace with glue. Add glitter.
Let dry. Trace with your fingertip.

Uppercase "R"

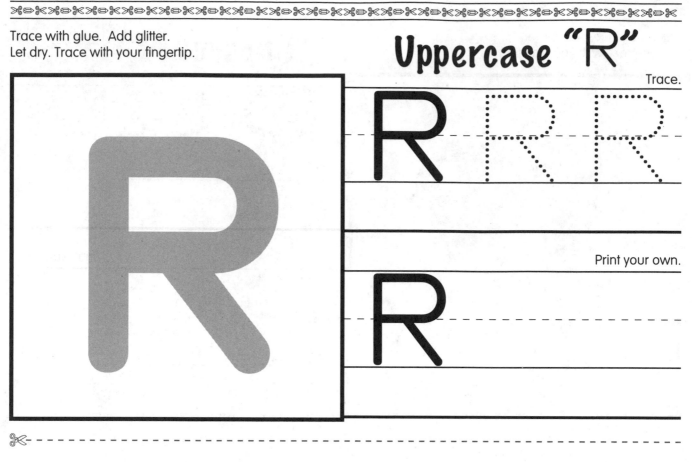

Trace.

Print your own.

Name

Trace with glue. Add glitter.
Let dry. Trace with your fingertip.

Lowercase "b"

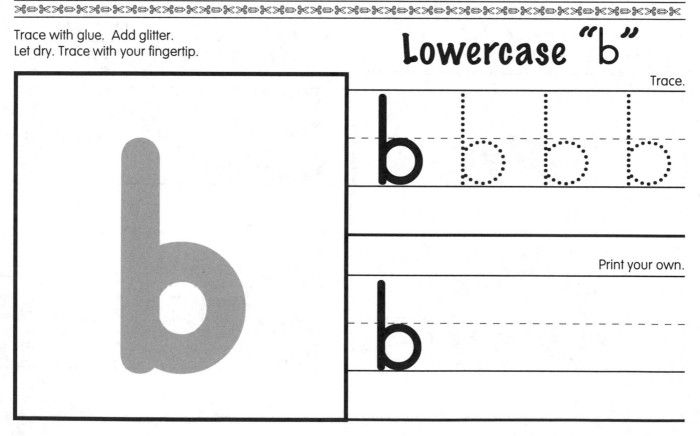

Trace.

Print your own.

Name

Trace with glue. Add glitter.
Let dry. Trace with your fingertip.

Trace.

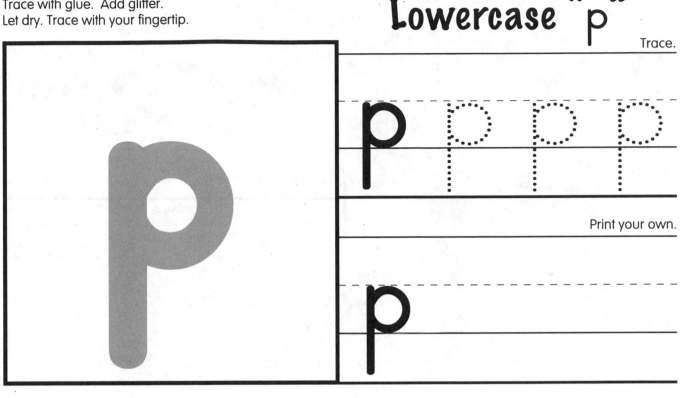

Print your own.

Name

Trace with glue. Add glitter.
Let dry. Trace with your fingertip.

Trace.

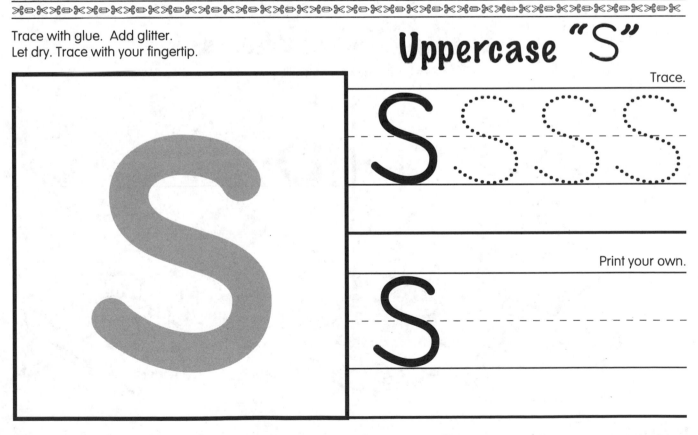

Print your own.

Smiling Curves

Directions: Practice drawing smiling curves.

✂ -

Name

Smiling Curve Waves

Directions: Practice drawing smiling curves.

Name

Trace with glue. Add glitter.
Let dry. Trace with your fingertip.

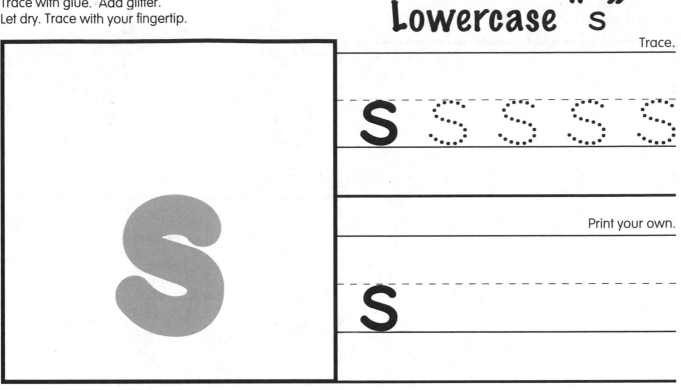

Trace.

Print your own.

Name

Trace with glue. Add glitter.
Let dry. Trace with your fingertip.

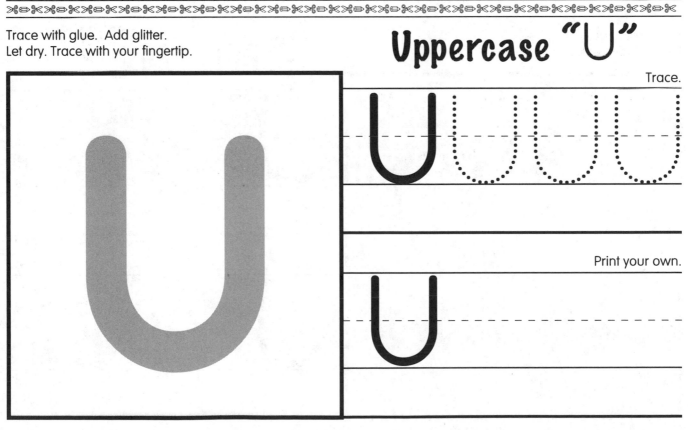

Trace.

Print your own.

Name

Trace with glue. Add glitter.
Let dry. Trace with your fingertip.

Lowercase "u"

Trace.

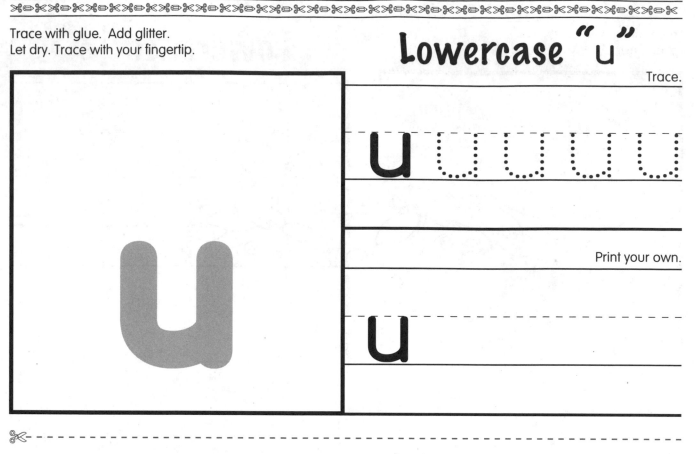

Print your own.

✂ -

Name

Trace with glue. Add glitter.
Let dry. Trace with your fingertip.

Uppercase "J"

Trace.

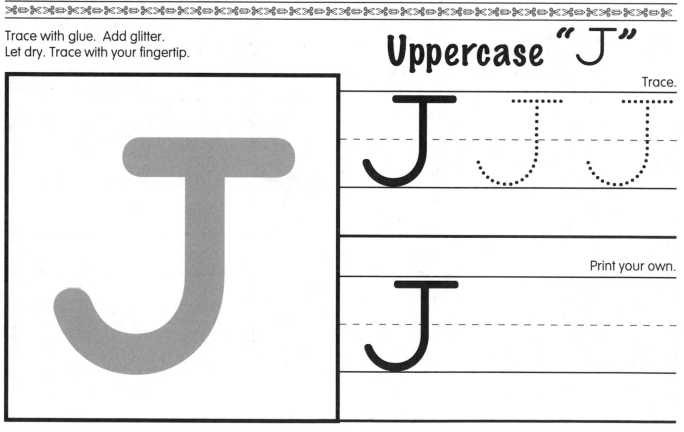

Print your own.

Frowning Curves

Directions: Practice drawing frowning curves.

✂ -

Name _____

Frowning Curve Jumping Frogs

Directions: Practice drawing frowning curves.

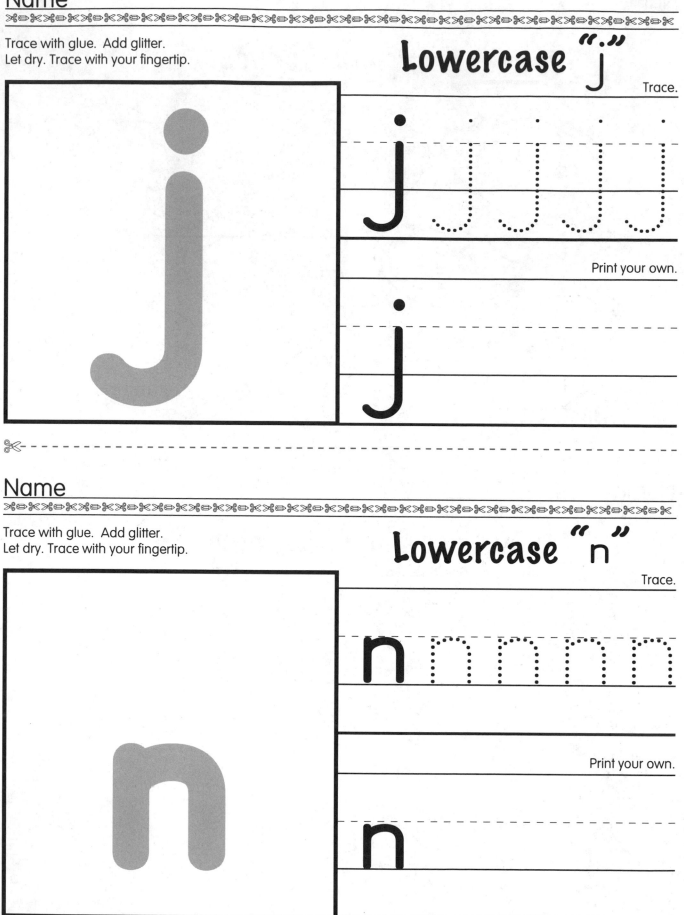

Name

Trace with glue. Add glitter.
Let dry. Trace with your fingertip.

Lowercase "j"

Trace.

j j j j j

Print your own.

j

j

Name

Trace with glue. Add glitter.
Let dry. Trace with your fingertip.

Lowercase "n"

Trace.

n n n n n n

Print your own.

n

Name

Trace with glue. Add glitter.
Let dry. Trace with your fingertip.

Lowercase "m"

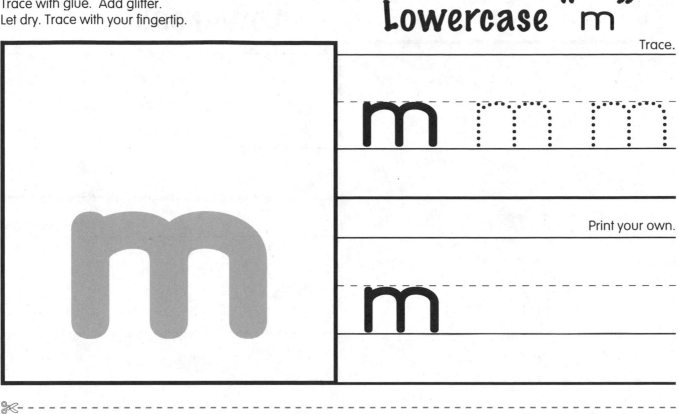

Trace.

Print your own.

✂--

Name

Trace with glue. Add glitter.
Let dry. Trace with your fingertip.

Lowercase "h"

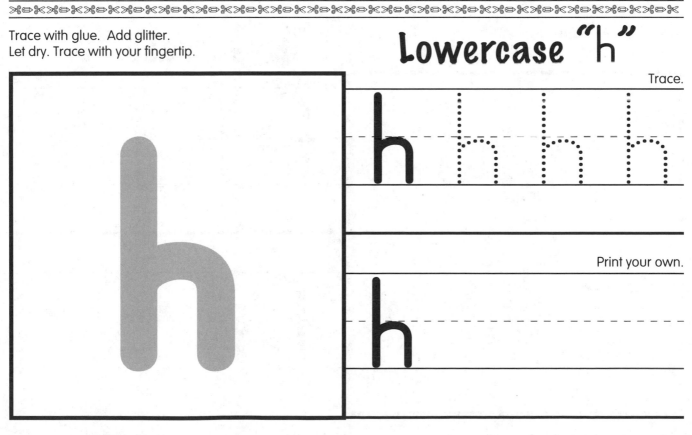

Trace.

Print your own.

Trace with glue. Add glitter.
Let dry. Trace with your fingertip.

Lowercase "r"

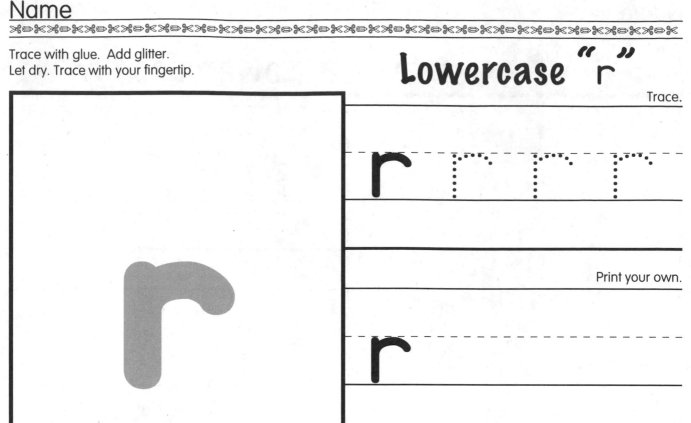

Trace.

Print your own.

Trace with glue. Add glitter.
Let dry. Trace with your fingertip.

Lowercase "f"

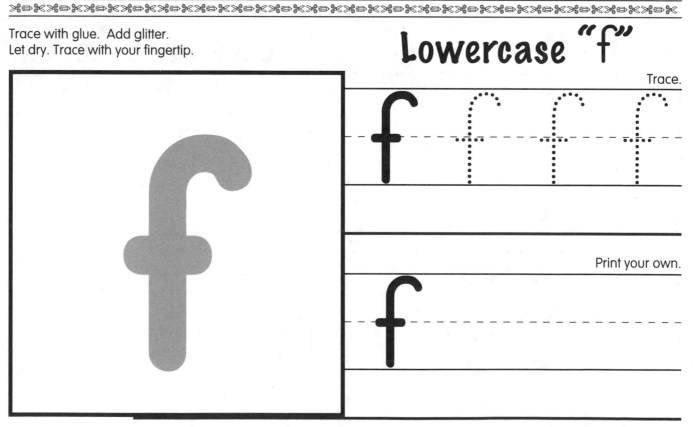

Trace.

Print your own.